House of Kahmanns

To Barb
with gratitude
and warm
wishes
Patsy Kahmann July 2023

House of Kahmanns

A Memoir

A story about family love and shattered bonds,
about finding each other in the aftermath

P. G. Kahmann

House of Kahmanns

Copyright © 2023 by Patsy Kahmann
ISBN: 978-1-957331-07-2

All rights reserved.

Published in the United States of America by
A to Z Letterpress, Montevideo, Minnesota

Book cover design by Jennifer Jones Nienabor
Front Cover house photo by Andy Kahmann
Special photo designs by Patsy Kahmann
Formatting and interior design by Andy Kahmann and
  Joy Minion/Minion Editing & Design, West Fargo, ND

Disclaimer: This memoir is a truthful recollection of actual events in my life. While all the stories are true, some names and identifying details have been changed.

Give sorrow words;
The grief that does not speak,
Whispers the o'er-fraught heart,
and bids it break.
— **Shakespeare**

Dedication

To Mom and Dad
I promised you I would write this story

CONTENTS

PROLOGUE	Welcome to Minnesota	i
CHAPTER 1	Building Walls	1
CHAPTER 2	Crossroads	17
CHAPTER 3	The First House	19
CHAPTER 4	My Kids	27
CHAPTER 5	The Sound-Off	33
CHAPTER 6	To the Airport	37
CHAPTER 7	Hated Babysitters	43
CHAPTER 8	Miss Millie Bea	47
CHAPTER 9	Dad's Boss	51
CHAPTER 10	The Bowling Boy	59
CHAPTER 11	Gentle Lies	69
CHAPTER 12	Ten Houses	77
CHAPTER 13	Birthday Candles	89
CHAPTER 14	70 Miles Away	91
CHAPTER 15	Mom Said	97
CHAPTER 16	Five by Five	99
CHAPTER 17	Andy's Hand	103
CHAPTER 18	The Envelope	107
CHAPTER 19	Almost Famous	113
CHAPTER 20	On the Move	121
CHAPTER 21	The Aftermath	125
CHAPTER 22	A Full House	131
CHAPTER 23	The Last House	143
EPILOGUE		153
POSTSCRIPT		155
ACKNOWLEDGMENTS		159

The Kahmanns, on the move to Minnesota

The Parents:
Jack Kahmann, 38
Della Kahmann, 38

The Children:
Karl, 13 — 8th grade
Patsy, 12 — 7th grade
Eric, 11 — 6th grade

Andy, 9 — 4th grade
John, 8 — 3rd grade
Paul, 7 — 2rd grade

Kevin, 5 — kindergarten
Katy, 4 years
Karen, 3 years

Phillip, 2 years
Jimmy, 8 months
Beth, yet to be born

PROLOGUE

We moved to Minnesota in the back of a pickup truck—my seven brothers and me. It was the end of summer 1962.
We were moving away from something—not towards.
That much I knew.
We were moving to a place we had only known in July, visiting Mom's family, swimming in their cold lakes and camping in a grove of pine trees that smelled like Christmas. We got to stay up late watching the dazzling dance of the Northern Lights.
But this trip would be different. It would be autumn soon.
We had heard tales of winter blizzards locking people inside their homes, pushing snowdrifts higher than the front door.
"Don't be ridiculous," Mom said and tried to soften our fears with the news that soon we'd have our very own ice-skating rink right outside the back door. "You'll learn to love winter, I promise."
We were city kids moving to the prairie because Dad's boss had decided to send his best salesman to the farmers of southwestern Minnesota. Dad was given a new pickup truck as his company vehicle.
There were eight of us kids in the back of the wide-open truck, nine if you count Pepper, our hefty German Shepherd, who weighed as much as a toddler.
We were squished in beside our honey-gold refrigerator—which Dad insisted on calling an icebox—and our overworked washing machine. They became our makeshift suitcases, stuffed inside with clean clothes and towels and diapers. Several layers of blankets and pillows filled the floor of the truck, making a gigantic bed for the ten hours to our new home.

i

Wedged up in the truck's cab was the rest of our crew. It was Missouri-warm in the late afternoon but Dad wore his felt fedora, a salesman's hat. He wore it for safekeeping. Mom flashed a half-smile at me through the cab window. She held Baby Jimmy, with our youngest sisters tucked in beside her.

Mom was barely pregnant with Baby #12, but only she knew it. Beth would be born the following March, making her and Mom the only true Minnesotans in our family of 14. The rest of us had the hills of Missouri in our blood.

It takes a long time to leave the loam of your birthplace behind, Mom would say, and I took it to heart.

Before we could officially begin our trip North, we had to make a short detour. We stopped to play tag with our Kansas City cousins and climb their apple trees. One last time. Minnesota seemed so far away from Aunt Helen's backyard.

"Now don't y'all start talking like those Yankees up North," Aunt Helen scolded. "You start talkin' funny I'll disown y'all. I mean it." She grabbed me and held me too tight.

"I promise, Aunt Helen, y'all don't have to worry about me. I'll never talk like that."

Gazing at our cousins' apple trees brought a cold disturbance in my chest. I was missing those trees and we hadn't even left yet.

CHAPTER 1
Building Walls

16 months later
January, 1964   Granite Falls, Minnesota

I hate January afternoons. If it had happened in the summer on a hot, muggy day, maybe I would hate July afternoons. But it didn't. It happened on a wintry afternoon when the sun no longer has anything left to give.

January brought blizzards and air so cold it made your tears freeze. One weekend it snowed and snowed and snowed until we couldn't see the barn. It was a perfect wet snow that you could pat and mold into a maze of walls and towers with windows.

On a normal day, the unfinished snowfort would have called us outside after school. We'd have been out there beside the barn where the drifts pile high, until Mom thought it was too dark and called us in for supper.

My brothers liked to create The Alamo. Karl and Eric fought over who got to be Davy Crockett. I pretended it was a castle. Karl and Eric and I would act like we were really building this for the younger kids. Andy was technically a younger kid, still in grade school, though he could act wise when he wasn't clowning around, so sometimes we would include him. Us older ones were in junior high school and didn't often play just-for-the-heck-of-it. Homework beckoned or chores called.

Still, when the snowdrifts were fresh and deep we couldn't help but join in their racket of war whoops and snowball fights. The prairie let us open up and shriek as loud as we needed to, without bothering anyone.

Six hundred acres of frozen fields lay between us and the nearest neighbors—one square mile of nothing. But it was a nothing that belonged to us.

The fields didn't belong to us and, technically, the barn didn't either. We were only renting the farmhouse. But Dad said: Nobody owned the sky. So we claimed it—all that empty space.

And how could we not be tempted by the barn? It was nestled in a stand of trees behind the house, sheltered slightly from the prairie winds. The barn hadn't been used since last fall when the farmhands had finished plowing the cornfields, stored the tractors for winter, and chained and padlocked the sliding timber doors. Until April it would be ours.

We respected the padlock. We knew it was meant to keep the barn doors from sliding open, to protect the machinery and hay bales from sleet and snow. But there was enough of a gap to squeeze through, allowing us to seek refuge when the winds grew too fierce, granting us precious minutes of afternoon shelter. Karl was the only one permitted past the front tires of the tractor. He kept his hunting rifle tucked behind a camouflage of hay bales, out of reach of younger hands. He was never far from that rifle, taking Pepper across the fields with him, scaring up pheasants and quail. Pepper belonged to all of us but she was really Karl's dog.

Karl, the oldest, was 14-going-on-40 that January. He liked to tell people he was born 100 years too late. After the fall harvest, when only remnants of bared cornstalks splotched the landscape, Karl would traipse through its aftermath, as if he were a mountain man finding his way back to the Ozarks.

The Alamo was completed that Monday afternoon, as completed as a snowfort could be. In southwestern Minnesota, a blizzard would alter the landscape in a hurry. Still, it felt finished for now. Eric tied a handkerchief around the barrel of Andy's toy rifle to mark the entrance. Mom had delayed dinner to let us finish. She even bundled up Baby Beth to come out in the frigid twilight to see our handiwork.

Dad turned on the barn's floodlight. "I think this fort will last till Easter," he said, "with the proper tending, that is. No one plays in the fort alone. You can make snowballs, but no tunnels. Is that understood? Eric, I'm putting you in charge. You will be the safety engineer. Examine the walls every day. Now, let's go eat. Who's hungry?"

The clamor of a dozen voices filled the space between the barn and the back door, filling up our prairie sky.

Tuesday morning came early, dark and frigid. Our parents had plans to drive Grandma and Grandpa Meldahl to Minneapolis, over 100 miles away. Grandpa had a doctor's appointment at the VA Hospital and wasn't supposed to be driving anymore. Mom scurried around trying to put her lipstick on without a mirror. She always seemed so nervous when her parents were coming. Dad was in the kitchen checking his watch against the kitchen clock. He liked to be right on time. I liked that, too, and felt for my watch on my left wrist, where it always was, even while I slept. Dad laughed at how I needed to set my watch five minutes ahead so I could be on time.

We both looked up as headlights from the driveway trailed across the cupboards. We could hear the crunch of tires on hard snow. I ran to the dining room window and watched Grandpa's big white 1957 Chevy stop just short of the front porch steps.

"That man is a menace behind the wheel," Dad muttered. "Somebody should take his keys away."

Grandpa honked the horn as he was getting out from behind the driver's seat. It was hard to tell if he did it on purpose or if his big fat belly had pressed into the horn and made it go off. Our dad didn't like anybody honking a horn at him, so he didn't rush any. Grandma was already sitting in the backseat. I could barely see her through the windshield; it was so frosty. But she had the brightest smile and it glistened even in the dark. I waved to her and she blew me a kiss. I could picture how it went: Grandpa ordering Grandma to sit behind the passenger seat even before they left their home in Hanley Falls, seven miles away.

Grandpa's cane steadied him as he worked his way slowly around the front bumper to the passenger side. Just as he got to the right headlight I saw him slide on a patch of ice and grab for the bumper. Karl was standing at the window next to me and saw it too. We started to laugh. "Big tub-o-lard."

"Karl!!" I said, "don't let Mom hear you say that." Grandpa only had one good leg so we shouldn't have laughed. But he was a scary man, with his wooden leg and grumpy voice.

Lucky for us Grandpa didn't fall because we would have had to go out and pick him up. Instead, he banged the bumper hard with his cane, blaming it for being in his way, like he blamed us for always being in his way.

It didn't make sense. No one had a sweeter grandma than we did. How could she put up with Grandpa?

"He's so crabby all the time," I said to Grandma.

Every morning she had to give him a shot for his diabetes and rub ointment on the stub of his thigh where his fake leg—a hollow, wooden tube with straps that wrapped around his waist—became a part of him.

It didn't look much like a leg. Quarter-sized holes, evenly spaced up and down each side of the unbending leg, caused an echoing sound when Grandpa would smack his cane against it, punctuating his reprimands. Sometimes he would guide the tip of his cane to the cuff of his pant leg and raise it enough to expose the holes. Then he would use the cane to scratch his fake ankle, complaining that it "itched like all get out."

Grandma simply smiled and said his bark was worse than his bite, "and wouldn't you be crabby if you had to have a shot every day?"

Maybe so. But she never saw him raise his cane at us kids behind her back.

I turned from the window to give Mom and Dad a hug and kiss goodbye. Dad slipped me an envelope with loose change in it for milk money at school.

"There's enough here for all the kids. Divide it up right before they get on the bus. Otherwise, you'll be looking for lost money. Mom's got all the lunches packed and on the counter. Karl, you know what to do. Don't forget Big Jim's medicine at noon."

Jimmy wasn't really big, but he had a deep voice for a two-year-old, the result of an operation that slightly damaged his windpipe. Dad rechristened him Big Jim and the name stuck.

"How come Karl gets to stay home?" asked Andy. I turned to Mom with the same question.

"Mrs. Brennen phoned this morning, sweetheart. I was counting on her to babysit, but she's sick. It'll be all right." Mrs. Brennen was a neighbor who had befriended Mom when we moved into the farmhouse the previous year. The Brennens farmed the land next to ours and were sort of outcasts. The townspeople judged how the farm families lived. We heard the Brennens were sometimes "on welfare." It didn't seem to bother Mrs. Brennen. She was the one who told us the rumors. She talked a lot and I liked her a lot.

Mom gave me a hard squeeze. I inhaled her perfume. She looked pretty in her bright pink sweater that matched her lipstick, but I didn't tell her. Mom stepped back and hesitated. I could tell she didn't want to go. Not yet.

"Give Beth a hug for me. I'd better not wake her. And, Karl, don't forget to strip the beds and get the sheets washed. It's Tuesday, you know."

Then Mom hurried outside. I watched as she opened the door behind the driver's seat. I couldn't see her anymore. The frosted car window looked like jagged glass.

Dad stood at the doorway and spoke to the younger kids, always his captive audience.

"You mind Karl today and do as he says. He's in charge. We'll be home by suppertime. Be good."

He grabbed his hat from the line of crowded coathooks on the porch, his soft Cavanagh fedora with its sharp crease down the middle. Dad had a ritual with his hat that I loved to watch, but on this day he skipped all that and was out the door. All I could see was Grandpa hogging Mom's place in the front seat and nothing seemed right. I heard Beth crying in the next room and knew she needed her diaper changed.

But something called to me on the porch, and I lingered, watching our father slide in behind the wheel so smooth and sure of himself. It's a good thing Dad is going to drive today. Our dad was a good driver, a very good driver.

Suddenly, I felt this urge to call Mom back for one last hug. It seemed like I needed to ask her something. I wasn't sure what. I only knew I wanted her back on the porch. Just for a minute. But Dad was impatient and he surely would have yelled. I only needed One. More. Minute.

It didn't make sense. They had left many times before and I had not felt this shakiness deep inside. We liked being in charge when they were gone, Karl, Eric, and I. We knew what to do.

I quickly looked around the porch, hoping Mom had left her scarf or gloves or anything I could run out to her. The snow-white Chevy taunted me through the broken screen of the porch door, reminding me of ... that dream. From last night. It woke me up, it was so real. I didn't get a chance to tell Mom about it, where I saw Pepper lying in front of Grandpa's car.

In slow motion in my dream I watched Karl crash through The Alamo crying out, "Pepper! Get up, girl. Please," and he buried his face in her matted fur.

I just wanted Mom to tell me again that dreams can't make things happen.

Even though they sometimes did. Like the time I dreamt I saw our Kansas City grandfather in a coffin. He had never been sick. But he died right after I had that dream.

I needed Mom to tell me the day was going to be okay. That Pepper would be alive when they got back home. That Karl wouldn't get in trouble for missing school.

That's it. That's what I felt uneasy about. Karl had never missed school to take care of the younger kids. I worried we would get in trouble if the principal found out.

I let them go without running out to the car. The headlights of Grandpa's Chevy blinked at me, Dad's signal goodbye. Beth cried again and I turned to soothe her. I didn't watch the taillights fading down the long, country road away from us.

There was much to do to get seven kids ready for the bus and the other four, too young for school, were demanding to be fed.

It was too cold to snow that January Tuesday, but the wind suddenly became so fierce it created a ground blizzard. I peered out into the white fog, straining to see the barn, wishing Grandpa's car would return. You could hear the wind screaming loudest by the bay window in the dining room.

Karl poured milk into four cereal bowls for the youngest ones. Andy rounded up the school kids, who were grabbing coats off the hooks.

"Come on, the bus is coming!" On most days when it wasn't blowing snow, we could see a patch of orange from across the cornfields, and we knew we had about three minutes before Mr. Vogel steered the bus into our driveway. We were the last stop and his turn-around point.

"It's almost 7:00," I hollered from the kitchen, poised to hand out paper bag lunches Mom had made the night before. She always personalized each one with her fancy penmanship.

"This isn't mine, it's Katy's," Kevin complained.

"Where's our milk money?" Paul demanded.

"I put it inside your lunch bag. It's blowing harder now and I don't want you losing dimes in the snow."

Eric had already cleared a path to the bus stop, propping the shovel in a snowbank to be retrieved on the return trip from school. But the fierce wind kept erasing his efforts.

It was my ritual at the end of the pathway to turn and wave at the little kids who were watching from the bay window. They always looked kind of sad, left behind. Especially Karen. She and Katy were a year apart in age, and until this year, had never been more than steps away from each other. Kindergarten took Katy away, and after school those two almost-twins could be found huddled in a corner where Karen would make Katy tell her what she learned.

Today I focused on the bus. Any second the headlights should have been turning into our driveway. But the ground blizzard took away our view of the long road.

Suddenly, a giant flash of orange slid past the driveway, stopping as the back end of the bus grazed the mailbox. Mr. Vogel opened the door and honked. "Hurry up."

"Single file," Eric shouted over the wind.

I picked up Katy and carried her to the front step of the groaning bus. She was missing a boot.

"We're late," shouted Mr. Vogel. Eric was the last to get on the bus, holding up Katy's snow-packed boot.

Now we were headed in the wrong direction and Mr. Vogel had to contend with a detour. The ground blizzard caused previously fallen snow to rise up and block the windshield of the school bus faster than its wipers could clear it. Old Vogel, as kids called him, suddenly seemed too frail behind the huge, flat steering wheel to keep the bus from wobbling and sliding as it veered down each country road. Old Vogel wasn't about to let a few snowdrifts beat his record. He took great pride in the fact that no student on his watch was ever tardy because of bad weather.

At the next corner I saw it before it happened, that he'd cut the turn too sharply and when he did, I grabbed for Katy who was sliding into the aisle away from me. The bus teetered back and forth. For an instant it seemed certain we would topple over.

How horrible for Mom and Dad. To be gone while us kids lay in that deep ditch, I thought.

This vision came at me of metal and snow. We hovered on the edge of the embankment for a long second, two wheels in the air. The bus bounced down on all fours, only to slide across the road into a snowbank.

His face red, Old Vogel clutched and shoved the wobbly gearshift into Reverse. Then to First. Back-forth, back-forth. Forward. We joined the momentum, rocking the bus, willing it forward, as tires spit out snow and ice and finally, gravel. The bus lunged free!

And just as suddenly the ground blizzard settled down. I looked at my watch—five minutes past seven. A cold breath blew across my face and I began to shiver.

An *accident*. That's what I heard. *Accident*. I looked around and heard it again. Distinctly. "There's been an accident." The words seemed to come from inside me. But it was not me saying them. It was a big voice inside my head.

I couldn't stop shaking. It didn't make sense. We were safe now in this big bus, and Old Vogel had eased up his frantic steering. But I couldn't stop the shivering.

All morning it was like that. Voices in my head. There's been an accident. Buzzing in my ears. Accident.

First period math class. I could see Mr. Unruh scribbling on the blackboard, turning, pointing to raised hands, punctuating his column of figures with a long piece of chalk. But I couldn't hear him through the droning. Louder and louder, like Phillip's tom-tom, it began to fill me up and take over.

Accident. Accident. Ac-ci-dent.

Second period class my desk was close to the radiator, but it didn't stop the shivering. Something was shaking me from the inside out. I felt my forehead with the back of my hand, like Mom would do when I had a fever and a shudder would come from deep inside my chest, fighting to get out. "It's just the chills, honey," Mom would say as she covered me with blankets. "It'll pass soon." Mommy, hold me. Wave upon wave, the tremors continued, until Mom would lie down, draping herself on top of me. "There ... there ... there," she'd croon over and over until finally the fever broke.

But not this time. I was on my own.

Third-period English class. Our assignment, silent reading. But for me, the words shimmered on the page. I yearned to close the book and set my head down. Just for a minute. To catch my breath. I could hear my heart beating. Fast. Too fast. It was hard to breathe deep enough.

The black intercom box behind the teacher's desk beckoned, reminding me of our telephone in the dining room, silent mostly, a fixture on the wall. Somehow, I knew it was going to ring soon, even though weeks could go by without alerting the teacher. Last night our telephone had startled us at suppertime. Dad never let anyone answer during dinner, but it had been silent for so long, even he seemed shaken by its ring.

"Yee...ellow." Dad bellowed his signature greeting into the mouthpiece, never saying Hello, like normal people do. He always stretched it out in his long, Kansas City drawl and made it sound like the color. "Certainly, you can talk to your daughter," he said to the air and handed the phone to Mom. Grandma must have paid our overdue phone bill, like she had done with last month's electric bill.

Dad's sales career had stalled. The farmers of southwestern Minnesota weren't so eager for his new way of feeding their livestock. But Mom was sure things would turn around in the Spring. That's how sales were, she'd say. Their trip to Minneapolis was also for Dad to meet with a businessman about a new venture. That's when our ship would come in, Dad would say.

"Five-thirty tomorrow morning. We'll be ready, Mother." Mom hung up the phone.

I sat in the middle desk of the middle row. In full view of the black box on the wall. Behind the teacher's desk. Waiting. Counting ... ten, eleven, twelve. Counting the floor tiles to the door as the thrumming filled the inside of my head.

Karl! Did Karl remember the telephone was working again? What if Beth had fallen off the bed when she was getting her diaper changed? She could squirm so. Had Big Jim's cough turned worse? Maybe he was choking like when he got croup. You had to prop him up with lots of pillows, so he could breathe after his coughing spells. Did Karl remember the telephone was working again? Please, Karl, remember. Phillip and Karen might have jumped too hard down the back staircase into the pile of laundry that was waiting to be washed that day. A volcano of sheets and blankets and pillowcases. I knew Karl would have had their help as he coaxed the kids and sheets off the beds, promising a parachute ride down the staircase. But Karl was Davy Crockett when he was in charge of the kids and nothing bad could happen under his watch.

... 13, 14. Faster and faster. Roaring rhythms inside my head. I tried to sit up straighter so I could breathe. Something was squeezing my chest. Tighter and tighter. How could I stop this? Mommy. Hold me.

Suddenly, a shrieking sound shattered the classroom. The intercom! It's buzzing jerked Miss Hannah's head. She practically tripped over her chair trying to grab the earpiece. Somehow, I knew it was my name she was going to call.

"Patricia, you must go to the principal's office. Right now." I had already stood up.

It was 14 tile steps to the door. Walking down the corridor I prepared myself for the encounter. I don't know how I knew these things ahead of time. I knew it wasn't Karl they were going to talk to me about. I had started to see a vision in front of me. Something was wrong with Mom.

Patsy? I heard Mom's voice right beside me, like the times I would wake up in the middle of the night with an earache and she would whisper the pain away. It was cold in the hallway and I hesitated as I passed my locker, wondering if I should grab my coat.

But ... wait a minute ... There, at the end of the corridor where three hallways converged, I really saw her!

Oh, thank you, God. I began walking faster as Mom came towards me. I was sure I caught a whiff of her perfume. When she was almost close enough for me to call out to her, Mom stopped abruptly and turned into the library. Why did she do that? I started to run, even though it was against the rules to run in school. Didn't she see me? I had my hand on the library door and I could see Mrs. Carlson through the window.

She wore the same pink sweater as Mom's.

My heart sank back into my chest, crushing me as I struggled to breathe. I turned once again toward the principal's office. The thrumming in my head had resumed. It was hard to navigate the hallway through the visions in front of me, a whirling blizzard of snow and metal.

My brother Eric, already seated outside the principal's door, whispered, "Do you think they found out about Karl? I bet he's going to get in trouble for missing school."

For a second I thought maybe I was wrong. Maybe it wasn't as terrible as the things I had been seeing. Hearing. The secretary escorted us into the principal's office and motioned for us to sit down. She left us in there with this stern-looking man as she closed the door behind her, carefully.

"Your parents were on their way to Minneapolis?"

"Yes, it was an emergency. They had to take Grandpa to the VA Hospital. For his diabetes. Grandma doesn't drive and Grandpa's not supposed to. And that's why Karl . . ."

"Your parents," the principal interrupted, "have been in an accident. They were hit by a truck. Your mother." He stopped and my world stopped.

"Your mother. Has been hurt bad. They don't know. If she will live. It happened around. Seven. This morning in. Norwood. That's about 70 miles from here."

The porch. If only I had called her back ...

"... a priest was with her and gave her the Last Rites."

... for just one minute.

"... we have no more details right now."

I couldn't bear to think past the next moment. I stared straight ahead behind the principal at the pure white snow outside his window. Mommy. Mommy. I'm sorry. This is all my fault.

"You kids might as well get back to class. There's nothing you can do." The principal stood up and directed us out into the quiet corridor and closed the door.

"How could they send us back to class? Do you think we should try to walk home?"

"It's too cold, Eric. We can't walk four miles in this."

"They only give the Last Rites to someone who is dying."

"I know."

We huddled in the hallway underneath the staircase. Eric pulled a rosary out of his pocket and we began to pray. "Hail Mary, full of grace. The Lord is with thee." We prayed as fast and as hard as we could until the lunch bell sent students into our sanctuary and split us up. For the rest of the school day I filled my head with prayers, trying to quiet the voices. How many Hail Marys will it take to save my mother's life?

Later that gray afternoon Karl, Eric, and I stood on the porch of our home when we should have been playing in the snowfort. Instead, we watched as strangers took our brothers and sisters away. One. By. One. Andy went in this car. Johnny went in that. I could not bear to look at them as they were placed in separate cars.

Behind us in the kitchen our nearest neighbors, Mr. and Mrs. Anderson, sat at the table. They were an elderly couple from down the road who joined us for dinner every Sunday. I heard them telling Father Buckley they wanted to come and stay with us kids to keep us all together. But the priest said, "No." The Andersons weren't Catholic. We all had to be placed in Catholic homes.

"You understand." No! I don't understand. But Father Buckley was the one in charge.

One. By. One. Children were ushered out the door. We never did anything One. By. One. We had been taking care of each other forever, always together. We had a buddy system. It was my job to look after Kevin and Phillip, with Andy's help. Karl and Eric each had their three buddies. How could I handle my mom dying and not have my brothers and sisters beside me?

Karl and Eric and I stood on the porch and watched them all leave. Next, they took Paul, then Katy and Karen. Phillip. Andy and Big Jim. Beth had already been snatched from her crib. Mrs. Brennen, sick as she was, had come earlier, before the church people got there, and took Beth home with her. For a few tense minutes Kevin went missing. I ran upstairs to his favorite hiding place. Karl took Pepper outside, where they finally found him behind the barn. Kevin was crying and cradling his new Christmas present, a shiny red truck. Karl burrowed a hole into a snowbank and helped Kevin place it inside. For safekeeping.

Beside me Eric began to shake and it was not from the January air. I knew about the shaking. He stood there feet planted firmly on the porch steps, his pantleg quivering. The biggest tear swelled at the corner of his eye and splattered down his cheek. I watched it in slow motion, catching on his shirt collar. It was the only one.

Mrs. Anderson cried quietly. Mr. Anderson stroked Pepper's soft fur, trying to keep her from growling at the strangers. "I promise I'll look after her," he said to no one really.

It all happened so fast, this shattering of our lives.

We had to be strong for the younger kids. We had to reassure them that Mommy was going to be all right, that Daddy was coming home soon, that Grandma and Grandpa were okay.

And then we had to send them off into unknown places.

How could these people think they would take better care of us—than us? They didn't know what time Phillip and Jimmy went to bed or the songs we'd sing. They didn't know what stories Katy and Karen begged Andy to tell. They didn't know that Paul and Kevin liked cinnamon toast for breakfast or that Johnny was the expert in making it just right. How could they know that Beth, at ten months old, would crawl out of her crib and snuggle the rest of the night beside me?

Karl, Eric, and I watched as another piece of us left the driveway in a procession of red taillights.

And this. This is all my fault. If only I had called her back.

One by one my brothers and sisters were being sent to good, Catholic homes. But how could these people nourish our souls? They didn't even know how we prayed.

In unison. Out loud. Every night before lights out:

"In the name of the Father, and of the Son, and of the Holy Ghost." Dad's solemn voice booming from the bottom of the staircase sounded like a priest at the altar. On cue, we would kneel beside our beds, making the sign of the cross.

"Now I lay me down to sleep," Mom would continue softly from one of our upstairs bedrooms. "I pray the Lord my soul to keep," Dad's loud voice bounced through the walls, as he ascended the steps.

Mom: "If I should die ..."

It was our part to answer: "... before I wake!" Dad's turn: "I pray the Lord ..." Us: "... my soul to take!"

"God bless ..." Dad would pause, signaling our response. "Daddy," came our answer.

"God bless ..." he would state, louder this time, "MOMMY," we shouted back, matching him.

"God bless ..." "KARL."
"God bless ..." "PATSY."
"God bless ..." "ERIC.
"God bless ..." "ANDY."
"God bless ..." "JOHNNY."

"God bless ..." "PAUL."
"God bless ..." "KEVIN."
"God bless ..." "KATY."
"God bless ..." "KAREN."
"God bless ..." "PHILLIP."
"God bless ..." "JIMMY."
"God bless ..." "BABY BETH."

"... anyone else?" Dad would ask, just to make sure we had covered all the bases.

"And God bless everybody in the whole wide world! Amen. Amen. AMENAMENAMENAMEN," a crescendo of voices swelled to fill up the house. That became our prayer, not the words so much, just that cloud of sounds bursting out into the night, punctuating our prairie sky.

Then Dad would begin singing, alone, softly, the old bugle call from his army days, which we had claimed as our nightly hymn: "Day ... is ... done. Gone ... the ... sun."

As Dad sang slowly, deliberately, Mom would begin tucking the youngest ones into bed, making sure everyone in some way got a piece of her, whether a soft kiss or a squeeze. My favorite was when she would stroke my cheek lightly with the back of her hand, right close to my ear.

"From the lakes ... from the hills ... from the sky." When he hit that last high note Dad's voice turned soft and faint, and the quivering timbre of it found its way down deep inside of my head anchoring me to my pillow.

"All ... is ... well," Mom would take over with her soothing soprano, "... safe-ly ... rest." On a good night Mom and Dad would end up standing next to each other, arms entwined, harmonizing the ending:

"God ... is ... nigh."

For one hushed moment the driveway lay before us, empty in the twilight. We were the oldest and we would be the last to go. I watched Karl take a rosary out of his pocket and carefully set it on the lid of the trashcan.

Reaching over to the line of nearly-empty coathooks, he pulled a knife from his hunting jacket, and shoved it deep in his pocket.

We stood at attention on the porch as they came for us, more headlights casting shadows on the walls of our frozen fortress. Karl's rosary began to lose its perch on the trashcan and the wooden beads, one by one, followed each other off the galvanized lid, slowly at first, then suddenly clattering to the floor in a heap.

We didn't speak. We didn't embrace. We didn't even look at each other. Eric pushed on the rickety screen door and stepped out into the night. Karl turned back to Pepper, hiding his face in her fur. I grabbed for the door handle and a wayward piece of broken screen caught my mitten, causing it to slip off my hand. I left it there, stuck on the porch door, waving to me, marking the spot where they came on a Minnesota January afternoon and took away the sky.

CHAPTER 2
Crossroads

Winter, 1964
The In-Between Time

It took a long time to piece together what happened that morning on a stretch of clear, unobstructed highway between Granite Falls and Minneapolis.

Much later, Dad would tell us he saw a vehicle, out of the corner of his eye, hurtling toward them, not stopping at the stop sign. He floored the gas pedal, hoping to outrun it. But the full force of the speeding vehicle hit directly behind the driver's seat, right where Mom was sitting. It propelled the Chevy down a deep ditch.

Dad would recall the details of the crash over and over, as if the retelling could soften the sound of the impact, could add one second and turn the battlefield on the highway into a scary close call. That it could erase the vision of his crumpled wife bloodied and unresponsive, could keep his kids from being flung out of his orbit.

Dad was ejected from the car and hit the pavement, never losing consciousness, he would insist. He could see Grandma and Grandpa lying on the highway. But he could not see Mom. The winter landscape and morning sun camouflaged the white Chevy. He noticed the other vehicle sitting peacefully nearby, he could hear the hiss of its draining radiator. Frantically looking for Mom, Dad slid down the snowy ditch, where he found it, the crushed car.

Beneath a pile of mangled metal, too heavy for Dad to lift, Mom was trapped. He struggled up the slippery hill and pounded on the driver's window of the other vehicle, pleading for help. The driver did not appear to be injured, but leaned away from the window and would not open the door. Later, when Dad discovered they were

17

two high school kids, he believed they must have been in shock. We would learn they were brothers who had been making early-morning bread deliveries for their parents' bakery.

The 16-year-old had a suspended license and was not the driver. His 14-year-old brother was, and suffered a broken nose. There were no tire marks on the pavement. The kid had run a stop sign and a yield sign and collided with the white Chevy.

Dad's army training kicked in, he would tell us, as he became laser-focused. He hurried back to Mom and with inexplicable strength pushed the chassis off of her. Most experts would tell you not to move an injured person, but Dad said he didn't want Mom dying in a ditch.

He carried her up to the highway where sirens could be heard off in the distance. I pictured him gently laying Mom down on the softer shoulder of the highway, beside Grandma. He draped his coat on top of both and used his handkerchief to stanch the bleeding at Mom's temple, picking razor shards of glass from her face.

The ambulance driver found a faint pulse; a nearby priest who had heard the crash rushed to the scene. Father Murphy gave Mom the Last Rites, a sacrament for the dying. He was certain she would not make it to the hospital in Glencoe, eleven miles away.

Dad begged the medic to tell him the truth.

"It doesn't look good, sir." They let him ride with Mom to the hospital. More ambulances arrived and took our grandparents and the other driver to the same hospital.

Dad waved off medical attention and paced outside the operating room until his legs gave out and he was forced into a wheelchair and finally a hospital bed. The small-town hospital found itself overwhelmed with the chaos of the accident victims. Doctors focused on stopping the bleeding from Mom's head and many deep facial lacerations. Her pelvis was shattered and left elbow twisted and limp, but they waited to do anything more than stabilize her, believing if she survived they would have to amputate her arm.

CHAPTER 3
The First House

Winter, 1964
The In-Between Time

"Your mother is dead."

When I stepped off the porch the night of the accident, there were two cars in our driveway—one for Eric and one for me. Eric had already gotten into the Wengert's car. Mrs. Wengert, a good friend of Mom's, ran up to me and gave me a big embrace. "I wanted to take you too. But Father said it's better that you go with the Grant family."

A man I had only seen in church was waiting by the back door of his car. He flicked a toothpick towards the barn and turned to me before opening the door. "We have a surprise for you!"

Johnny!

Johnny was huddled against the opposite door. I couldn't make out what the man was saying, something about a mix-up and they had to drive all the way back from town. All that mattered was that my brother was in this car and I was not alone with these strangers. Johnny moved his bookbag so he could sit right beside me.

"So, Johnny, you happy to see your sister?"

"His name is John," I said. Months ago Johnny had told us not to call him that anymore.

"Johnny is for babies. I'm not a baby," he said. I tried to honor his wish, but we'd been calling him Johnny since he was born. Eight years was a long time to get used to something. He didn't seem to mind when I'd slip up and call him Johnny, but no one else could.

We rode to the Grant's house in the wide backseat of their fancy car without speaking. They tried to talk to me.

19

"Now, what grade are you in? Patty, is it?"

I had never been this rude before. When adults spoke to me, I answered.

But something made me instantly dislike this man.

"She's the same age as your brother's kid Connie," said the lady in the front seat. "So, eighth grade?" I didn't speak. "We have another surprise for you when we get home." I wasn't going home. The voices in my head were gone, taken over by outside sounds. Tires crunching on the frozen gravel. The hum of the car's heater.

And then the tick, tick, tick of my watch. The one Mom had given me for my tenth birthday. The one I had worn every day, winding it up each morning careful not to wind too tight.

I couldn't see it in the darkness of the Grant's car, the second hand of my watch but I could hear how it ticked off the numbers, pausing slightly and then starting again at each notch. Just like a heartbeat. Mom's heartbeat. I put my hand over the face of my watch and felt the pulsing in the palm of my hand. It was soothing. As long as I could feel the heartbeat of the watch, Mom would live.

Then I felt the weight of Johnny's head press into my shoulder. He took a deep sigh. For a moment I felt calm enough to breathe.

Beth! Oh, no. Where was Beth! I didn't remember seeing Beth when I came home from school. What if everyone forgot about her? What if she was hiding underneath her crib?

I broke my silence. My only power. "We have to go back. We forgot something."

"I'm sure it can wait. We have everything you need. And tomorrow we'll go shopping for some new clothes. How's that?"

"It's my sister! She's been left behind. I just know it. I didn't see her!"

"Now, now. I'm sure Father took care of everyone. But I'll give him a call when we get home."

"She likes to hide."

I knew this lady was wrong. I just knew it. I could always feel Beth with me. Even at school I would sometimes close my eyes and I could picture my baby sister crawling around the edges of the area rug in the living room. She didn't like touching the carpet. It stopped her like an invisible fence. But I couldn't remember seeing her in the chaos of the afternoon. What car took her? Where was she? I closed my eyes and like a movie screen I could picture every car that left the driveway—Katy and Karen left together. So did Andy and Jimmy. But Beth wasn't in the picture! How could I have missed her grabbing my hair and kissing my nose, and giggling when I called her *Baby Buckwheat*? I couldn't feel her, like I couldn't feel Mom.

In the backseat of the Grant's car breathing had become complicated again. I could feel my heart pushing through my chest. I gulped and gulped, trying to reach deeper for air. It felt like the time I got hit by a baseball bat that caught me square in the stomach.

On my lap lay Mom's ivory hanky that I had taken, moments before, from her Sunday coat. The one she used right before church to blot her lips. It carried her musky lipstick smell. I threaded one end through my watchband as I had seen Grandma do with hers. I buried my nose in my wrist and the distinctive fragrance helped me breathe.

The tires changed their tune as we drove over the bridge with the frozen river underneath. We were close to town. I kept breathing through Mom's handkerchief. As we drove past St. Andrew's Catholic Church I pressed hard on the face of my watch. I counted the pulses. The counting, the pulsing distracted me.

We drove straight towards Granite Falls High School at the end of the block and turned sharply to the left. Two blocks farther we came to a stop.

"Here's our house." The woman said. I noticed a huge letter **G** on the front door.

"You'll be surprised!" Mr. Grant said as he opened the car door.

We stumbled up the front steps, burdened with our bookbags and a paper bag with our pajamas. Once inside Mr. Grant paid the babysitter, a high school girl I recognized.

We were told where to hang our coats and where to wash our hands. "After that, join us in the kitchen." Johnny stayed by my side and we found the bathroom. The light was so bright it hurt your head.

Mr. Grant was waiting outside the bathroom door. "Took you long enough. We are waiting to show you the surprise."

One of the Grant kids came around the corner and shoved a kitten in my hands. "We thought you might like to pet the new addition to our family."

The cat clawed my hand and I dropped it. I did not like cats.

The Grant's house was lit with bright lights in every room, especially the uncluttered kitchen, which showcased sparkling countertops.

I was grateful when Mrs. Grant said it was bedtime. I'd be sleeping on a daybed next to their baby's crib. Johnny clung to me, and I asked if he could stay with me, but Mrs. Grant wouldn't hear of it. "We don't share beds in this house," she said. Mr. Grant took Johnny to the next bedroom with their youngest son. I followed them and watched from the doorway, wanting to say goodnight to my brother.

"So, Johnny, did you like the surprises?"

"His name is *John*," I said sternly to this man.

"The baby needs the lights out, so why don't you go to bed, Patty."

"My name is not *Patty*," I said under my breath.

"John, you take the top bunk," he ordered. I put my pajamas on in the dark and lay down on the stiff bed. I was used to reading myself to sleep but sleep was not on my mind. We were a praying family and with my rosary in hand, I had promised I would pray for Mom all night. I needed to get started.

The white, starched sheets scratched my cheeks and made me think of Dad's shirt collar. I longed for the comfort of my own bed with Grandma's frayed quilt and my mismatched sheets, yellowed from our rusty well-water.

I worried about Johnny in the top bunk. He had never slept in a bunkbed. I was afraid for him.

Now I lay me down to sleep, I began in my head. *God bless Mommy. God bless Johnny. God bless Mommy.*

The baby woke me up with her fussing. It was so dark in the room. The cries reminded me of Beth. *Where was my baby sister?* Mr. Grant was in the hallway with a flashlight. I wanted to have the courage to ask him about my sister. But I kept quiet.

I don't remember falling back to sleep but I awoke with a stabbing pain in my neck and pulled something away from my skin. My rosary. How could I have slept on it? No! How could I have slept at all? I rubbed the spot on my neck where the crucifix had left a mark. Thoughts of Mom crept around the edges. I had to keep my thoughts contained, focused on what was in front of me. What lay on the other side of thinking—being motherless—was too frightening to deal with.

I hurried to get dressed in the same clothes from the day before.

Breakfast in the Grant household was a silent affair, everything timed precisely. Mr. Grant had a soft-boiled egg that took just minutes to cook. The Grant children had orange juice first and then hot cereal with milk and honey. Mrs. Grant even sliced bananas to put on top of the cereal, something I had only seen on a cereal box. We ate our bananas right from the peel. Mrs. Grant was too busy to eat.

No one mentioned my mom and I was afraid to ask if they knew anything. I couldn't wait to get out of this ordered house and on to school. I had to find Eric and Karl.

"It's very cold today. Mr. Grant will drive you children to school." I couldn't wait. I grabbed Johnny's hand and we walked out the front door, heading in the direction I hoped was right.

I could see ahead of me the large stone letters, G F H S—Granite Falls High School. I walked Johnny to the elementary school and hugged him at the door. Then I ran to the high school and stood at the front, checking each bus as it drove up the semicircle driveway. Students seemed to stare at me and then move away. What if they know something I don't? What if they've heard something about Mom?

The tardy bell rang before I could get to Science class. The hall monitor sent me to the principal's office for a tardy slip. My very first one. The secretary took a long time signing her name on the form. Does she know something about Mom? I didn't have the courage to ask.

After each class I scanned the halls for Karl or Eric but I couldn't find either one. I decided after fourth hour to run to the cafeteria. I didn't care if running was against the rules.

The halls were crowded but I pushed my way through. Karl and Eric were both waiting by the cafeteria doors. We huddled close together. "Have you heard about Mom?" Eric whispered.

Fear grabbed me again. "No. Tell me she's okay. Tell me she's not dead," I begged.

Both Karl and Eric shook their heads. "We haven't heard anything. No one will tell us *anything*," said Karl.

"But yesterday Mrs. Brennen thought Mom was dead. She told me so. For an hour I thought Mom was dead. Until the Andersons came and said that wasn't true."

One of the lunch ladies brought us lunch trays and pointed to an empty table. "Mrs. Wengert called the hospital last night but they wouldn't tell her anything. Said they didn't have any news."

"I thought Dad would have been here by now. That's not good." And then I remembered. "Karl, where is Beth? I didn't see her yesterday."

"She was the first to go. Before you got home. Mrs. Brennen just picked her up out of her crib and took her. She'll be okay there."

"Where are the others? We need to talk to them." I opened up a notebook and wrote every name.

"I can run over to the grade school after last period and check the buses," said Eric.

"Karl, where are you staying? I'm at the Grants but I don't even know which Grants. I don't know their phone number."

"I'm at Joe Riley's house. Eric, you'll have to get Mrs. Wengert to keep calling the hospital. She's a nice lady. See if she can talk to Dad."

"Eric, I think the Grants live a few blocks from Wengerts. I'll look for you when I walk home tonight."

≈

Years later I would learn more details about that day Karl stayed home from school. I would learn that Karl had fed the four youngest kids their lunch. That he left the dirty dishes on the table with the breakfast dishes, like he had left dirty clothes and bedsheets in the back staircase, figuring he had all afternoon to do the laundry. He planned to wrangle the rest of us into helping him after we got home from school. Everything would be orderly and clean by the time Mom and Dad got home.

Karl and the kids had made a tent-town of blankets in the living room. That's where they all lay down for the afternoon nap. Beth was already asleep in her crib. Karl read to Karen and Phil and Big Jim until they all fell asleep. He fell asleep with them.

Suddenly, the back door banged open. Mrs. Brennen ran in screaming, "There's been an accident." She bent over Beth's crib and began wrapping her in a blanket. Mrs. Brennen sobbed, "Your mother is dead. Your father is bad." And then she ran out the door with Beth. Karl watched her lay Beth down on the front seat beside her. Then Mrs. Brennen ran back up the porch steps and leaned in the doorway.

"I don't know about your grandparents. Father Buckley will be here soon. He's getting people ready to take you kids."

She ran back to her car and the screen door banged in the wind. Karl latched the door and then wandered around the dining room staring at the phone on the wall. He wanted to call the one adult he felt closest to: Aunt Helen. But she was 500 miles away and he didn't know her phone number. He picked up the phone to hear the dial tone. Karl knew when it wasn't working, money was tight. It definitely was working today, but he had no way to use it.

For an hour Karl paced the floor, thinking Mom was dead. Until our nearest neighbors, the Andersons, came to the door and assured Karl it wasn't true. The accident was true, but they had just called the hospital and so far no one had died.

≈

I couldn't find Eric after school so I walked alone to the Grants. Mrs. Grant was in the kitchen making dinner. Johnny was at the kitchen table with his schoolbooks. He ran up to me and we held each other.

"John, back to the table. Homework gets done before dinner. Patty, go wash up. You need to eat early so you can go to Religion class tonight."

"My name is Patsy," I whispered.

CHAPTER 4
My Kids

Winter, 1964
The In-Between Time

"My kids are missing! God dammit! Where are my kids!?" Dad screamed into the phone. He had returned to our house the day after the accident. An empty house. "Where have they taken my kids?" he cried into the phone.

We would learn much later what had been happening in a hospital 70 miles away. Dad hovered at Mom's bedside, studying the flurry of activity as doctors and nurses rushed in and out. Specialists were called in, lots of whispers. Mom was taken back to the operating room. Her chart listed her in very critical condition. But he knew that. Grandma and Grandpa were together in a room down the hall, both in serious condition.

At daybreak Dad collapsed from dehydration and was put on a gurney and hooked up to an IV. A few hours later when he couldn't get a doctor to release him, Dad ripped out the IV and returned to Mom's bedside. She remained in a deep coma. Unable to help Mom, Dad felt compelled to get to us kids. That Wednesday afternoon, over the hospital's objection, Dad walked out to Father Murphy's car. He had convinced the priest, who had come to the scene of the accident, to drive him home to Granite Falls.

Instead of a houseful of kids, Dad found our dog pacing inside our empty house.

Father Murphy called the police and Dad grabbed the phone. "God dammit, what have they done with my kids?" Father took the phone from Dad and talked to the sheriff about meeting in town at Father Buckley's rectory.

Religion classes were taught every Wednesday night for the junior and high school students in all the churches in town. Karl and Eric were waiting for me on the steps to the church basement. No one had given us any word on our parents. I couldn't shake this feeling that Mom was dying. I remember having that feeling one other time when I was ten. The first person I knew to die was Pop, my beloved grandfather.

Pop was our Dad's dad. Everybody in the world called him *Pop*, and everybody thought the world of him. He made you feel like an expert at something. Every time I saw him, he'd teach me a card trick. He'd let me try it over and over and over, never rushing me, never losing patience. "Look at us. What a team we make," he beamed. One day towards the end of third grade I came home from school to see Dad holding the phone, crying. Pop was never sick. But now hushed voices surrounded us, Dad on the phone to his sister Helen. We heard words like: *pneumonia, lung cancer,* then *The Last Rites.*

I wanted to talk to Pop so bad I could hardly stand it. But there was nowhere I could go to escape this torment.

Homesickness.

That's what Dad called it when he found me wandering around Pop's empty house after the funeral. "It's the worst sickness there is, sweetheart, because no medicine in the world can fix it."

Dad knew firsthand about homesickness. He told us about the first time he felt it. He was six years old. It was Thanksgiving Day and they took his mother away from him. He never really got her back.

She had been descending into "a cave of madness," he called it. "One day she was the life of the party, the next day she couldn't get out of bed." The staying-in-bed part could last for months at a time. Pop tried to manage it all, the kids, his business, his beloved erratic wife. Until the day he couldn't.

Dad was sent to live with Grandfather Horigan, his mom's father, an eccentric mean old man. Dad's mom remained hospitalized for a year. She came home the day before Thanksgiving but she wasn't the same. Electric shock treatments had left her barely able to speak.

Dad would retell this story at Thanksgiving before Pop and Granny came for dinner. There was no word for bipolar at the time but he wanted us to understand why Granny was so quiet and nervous in our noisy house. He reminded us to be especially thankful we had each other. He knew what it was like to be wrenched from the only home he had known, to miss his mom in the middle of the night, to yearn for his beloved dog.

And now we were living Dad's own childhood nightmare.

Karl, Eric and I lingered in the doorway of the religion classroom. Father Buckley hadn't yet arrived to teach the class. At the far end of the basement corridor we saw an altar boy running towards us, his cassock billowing behind him. It had to be bad news. Another teacher scolded him for running. It was against the rules.

"But ... but. There's a bloody man over there. I seen him. Father Buckley says the Kahmann kids have to come. Right now."

We followed the boy next door to the rectory, the priest's house. Dad was standing in the small vestibule and he grabbed for us in a desperate embrace.

"How could they? How could they do this to you?" Dad sobbed.

"Mom! How's Mom!" we cried in unison.

"I don't know how I can go on without her."

"Is ... Mom ... Dead? Daddy?!"

"We don't know. We just don't know. I've been by her side but she doesn't move. They say she's in a deep coma. I wait for her to take her next breath. I just don't know what I will do without her."

Our arms could not hold him up and Dad sank to the floor.

"She's broken in so many places. They don't think she will make it another night. We need a miracle. You have to pray like there's no tomorrow."

Hail Mary, full of grace. On the floor with our father we prayed as he wept. We tried to help Dad to his feet but his legs could not hold him up. "I'm so sorry for what they've done to you kids."

The sheriff summoned an ambulance and Father Buckley told us to go back to religion class. But Dad was squeezing my hand so hard I could not let go. We ignored Father and waited until the ambulance arrived. Eric tried to button Dad's torn coat, which was stained with blood. Was it his? Was it Mom's?

The ambulance driver told us he couldn't take Dad back to the Glencoe hospital, it was out of his jurisdiction, but he and the sheriff helped lift him into the backseat of Father Murphy's car. Sweat was pouring from his forehead; his hand was shaking when I let go. That night in the Glencoe hospital doctors discovered Dad's back was broken.

The past beats inside me
like a second heart.
— **John Banville**

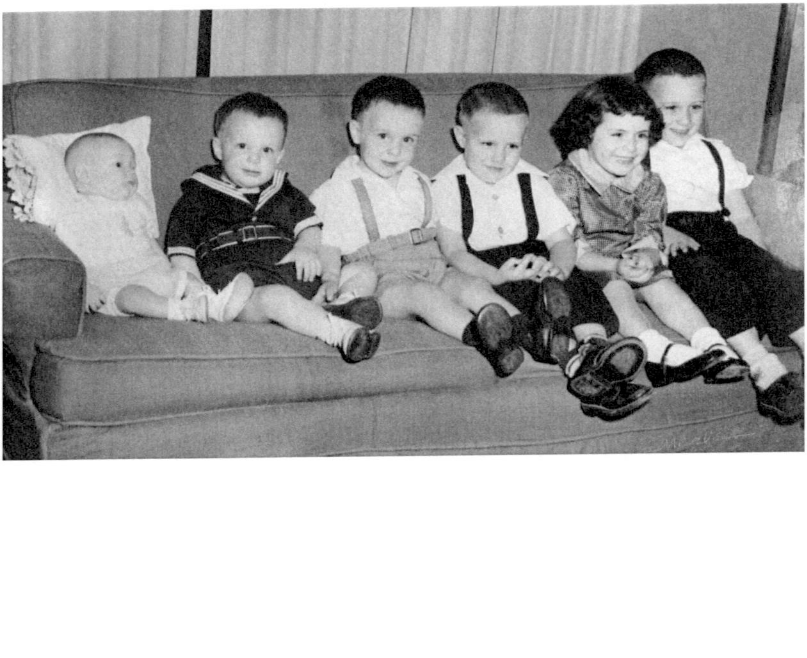

CHAPTER 5
The Sound-Off

1957 Kansas City

We had already gone a mile or more from Cottonwood Lake when The Sound-Off got as far as Johnny.
"Karl?"
"Here."
"Patsy."
"Here."
"Eric."
"Here."
"Andy."
"Present."
"Johnny."
"Johnny?"
"... goddammit, John, answer me."

I don't know how he did it, but Dad kept the car on the road as he turned his whole upper body around, straining to see through the clutter to the back of the station wagon, searching for my brother, steering without looking. Convinced that Johnny wasn't hiding under blankets or teasing with his silence, Dad shot back around to the front, clenching the steering wheel, barely hitting the brakes and expertly crossed one hand over the other, turning the steering wheel to the left, to the left, to the left, until the long, blue station wagon swiftly turned in the direction from which we had just come.

Dad's worst fear had now come to pass and I looked out of the side window at the blur of trees. One of us had been left behind. Nothing in the car moved, but everything outside whooshed by at a hundred miles an hour. We must have been flying slightly above the pavement.

I tried to relax into those few minutes of calm, willing from my mind the picture of my brother at the bottom of the lake. My ponytail dripped lake water down my back and I began to shiver. Karl looked over at Eric, and Eric looked at me, and I looked back at both of them. Guilt welled up between us, forming a triangle. We were responsible for each other. This never happened. It was never supposed to happen.

Dad's panic reached all the way to the back of the station wagon as he slammed on the brakes, threw the gearshift into park while we tumbled forward into one another.

Karl recovered first, jumped out of the open back window and followed Dad through crowds of people to the water's edge.

"Johnny! Johnny, where are you? JOHN DAVID KAHMANN. Answer me!" Dad's voice boomed above the squeals of summer.

Like a gunshot, his voice stilled all others. Stopped everything. Except.

Out in the middle of the lake.

All eyes turned to the only motion interrupting the stillness. A big, black innertube slowly turning around to the left, to the left, to the left, in a circle of oblivion. Three-year-old Johnny lay across the innertube, his chubby legs barely reaching the water, with one hand rhythmically cupping at the waves, making himself go round and round, getting further and further from shore.

"Judas H Priest," Dad growled. "How'd he get out there?" Karl took a running dive into the lake. I think he grazed his face on the sandy bottom because it was really too shallow to dive in like he did. But when Dad hollered, "Judas H Priest," it required an emergency response.

Johnny didn't even look up until Karl's furious crawl splashed him in the face and flipped the innertube and he slid under water. Karl yanked him back up, just long enough for Johnny to suck in some air before sending him down again.

We older ones were going to be in big trouble. Besides The Sound-Off to keep track of each other, we also had a buddy system. Johnny was on Karl's team. It was Karl's mission to teach him a lesson.

He shoved the innertube at Johnny, who grabbed on for dear life. Many grateful eyes watched their progress toward shore. Karl pushed the innertube forward with each overhand stroke, sometimes yanking it back, making Johnny drink the lake.

When they reached the shallow part, Karl grabbed Johnny's hand and forced him to walk faster than he normally would have. Dad didn't say a word and no one else dared to. When they got to the car, Dad smacked Johnny's wet bottom and pushed him into the front seat and slid in beside him. Dad turned around, glaring at us in the back. Mom counted heads, sternly whispering to Karl: "Was that display out there really necessary?" But then she noticed his cheek and reached for her handkerchief, dabbing at the blood.

We had never experienced such total silence. It was worse than the time Dad reprimanded us when Paul fell out of his highchair. Our cousins Jeannie and Joannie, older by several years, were babysitting and found Dad's liquor cabinet. It was their idea to put gin in Paul's fruit cocktail. But Dad held us responsible.

This ride home broke all barriers. Even the littlest ones knew better than to squirm. Finally, we reached the last hill and the streetlight illuminated our final turn: 74th Street Northeast. Pepper's frantic welcome broke the silence from a-half-a-block away. Her bark seemed louder than ever as she raced back and forth along the cyclone fence straining to greet us.

"Karl Edward, Patricia Gail, Eric Christopher. To the porch. The rest of you, to the tub. Andy, you fill it up. Make sure they wash that lake water off good."

Mom herded the rest of the kids up the porch steps, past us, and into the house.

Dad looked at each of us intently. One by one. His disappointment hurt more than a spanking. I wish he would have reprimanded us in the car. It would have been easier than facing him.

"After that incident with Paul. And now this. I am so disappointed in you. Y'all know what it means."

We nodded our heads and slowly walked up the steps and into the house. We knew. This would wipe out any responsibility we had earned, any chance of being our own babysitters.

Every single Saturday night Mom and Dad went out to dinner and every single Saturday night we had to have a babysitter. We knew we were old enough to take care of ourselves, Karl, Eric, and I. We had been changing diapers since we were five. Mom had been hinting lately that we might not need a babysitter every time she and Dad went out to dinner. It would only be for a couple hours; they would leave early and be home before dark. With Mrs. Mathis across the street, we could handle anything that might crop up. But that was before Johnny got left behind at the lake and other events conspired to prevent us from proving we were old enough.

What happened today was never supposed to happen. We would always humor Dad with his silly Sound-Off.

"Karl."

"Here."

"Patsy."

"Here."

"Eric."

"Here."

"Andy."

"Present."

"John."

"Here."

"Paul."

"I'm heeere," Paul would state proudly now that he could talk.

"Kevin."

"He's here, Dad," I would sigh and look at Mom holding Kevin to her breast.

"All present and accounted for," stated Karl.

"Kevin makes seven," Eric added.

"Good," said Dad. "Now, let's get this show on the road."

CHAPTER 6
To the Airport

1957 Kansas City

Every time we went somewhere as a family. After church. On the way back. To Granny and Pop's. On the way back. To the lake for a picnic. On the way back. Five or six of us—more as the family grew—would scramble into the station wagon where the back seat was always folded down, forming a massive metal bed for all of us to play on. There were spaces between the front seat and the back where we could tuck in paper bags filled with picnic lunches. Along the side near the car doors we stuffed deflated inner tubes and blankets and towels monogrammed with the name of the hotel Dad's latest trip had taken him to.

My favorite place was right in the middle where I could lean over and rest my arms and head on the front seat. The two youngest kids sat up in the front seat, one in Mom's soft arms, the other usually standing next to Dad's shoulder, helping to make sure we got where we were going. Except when a diaper needed changing and Mom would pass one of the babies back to Karl or me or Eric. And then it would be a scramble to see how fast we could find a dry diaper, trying not to lose the big yellow safety pins, trying not to stick the baby as he squirmed around enjoying his nakedness.

The Monday morning after our trip to the lake we were on our way to the airport. Dad was a traveling salesman and his job took him on the road every week. But "on the road" usually meant "in the air."

On Monday mornings we would all pile into our blue station wagon to help Mom drive him to the airport where he would catch an early flight to some big city, usually New York.

Dad hated to fly and this drive to the airport was one of the rare times he would allow someone else behind the wheel. Mom drove and we prayed.

The rosary was Dad's focus as he mangled the beads between tight fingers.

"*I believe in God, the Father Almighty, creator of heaven and earth.*" Dad would begin the first prayer of the rosary as we crossed the Paseo Bridge leading into downtown Kansas City where the airport was tucked into a slice of land right next to the Missouri River.

"The S.O.B. who designed this airport should be arrested," Dad would say when the weather looked dicey. "There's not a foot of tolerance. One of these days ..."

"Ja-a-ck. That's enough. I don't need you to leave me with Patsy and her nightmares. KCMO is a perfectly safe airport," Mom turned to me. "Why, when I was in stewardess training they told us: '*right next to the water is a great place for an airport.*'"

Sometimes the sign for the TWA concourse appeared before we had finished the last *Hail Mary*. It was up to us kids to keep the cadence of the prayers going while Dad gave Mom a lingering kiss goodbye.

Dad's boss, Harv Ringheim, would be waiting by the main doors to the terminal. "Look alive, Kahmanns," Mr. Ringheim would holler and he'd toss a silver dollar over his shoulder in our direction. Karl usually got to it first and we'd argue all the way home as to how we were going to spend it. A futile argument. It always ended up in Mom's cuss cup, which was mostly filled with Dad's coins because of his salty language.

"Harv, let's get this show on the road," Dad would say to his boss as he led the way through the terminal doors with an unlit cigarette between his lips. Dad was always the boss, even to his own boss, and the sooner he could get the plane to New York the better.

Mr. Ringheim liked to tell us a story about Dad's flying phobia. It was on a trip to Manhattan, with a stopover in the middle of Pennsylvania, where there were small mountains that added bumpiness to the takeoffs and landings. "Your father, Jack Kahmann, best salesman in the whole goddamn company. He's usually Mr.

Cool-as-a-Cucumber but he was not himself on that trip. Why, he was drinking whiskeys like they were going out of style."

Airplane travelers wore their Sunday best and Dad, like all the other men, had on a suit and tie. "Somewhere over the mountains of Happy Valley, Pennsylvania," Mr. Ringheim would explain, "your father takes off his suit coat." His crisp, white shirt had become drenched in sweat and Dad didn't want the suit coat to get stained. Our dad perspired like no one else. Even in winter, droplets would pool on his face and he'd curl his index finger at the top of his brow, swiping beads of sweat to one side of his forehead. Then he'd look for one of us kids or the dog, and with a pronounced snap of his wrist, fling his sweat across the room. Mom hated it; we loved it.

At this point in the story, Dad would take over the telling. "I have a pencil in my shirt pocket and Harv here reaches over to grab it."

Mr. Ringheim would interrupt. "Now, kids, you know you shouldn't have a pointed object, like a sharpened pencil, sticking out of your pocket. Right?" We would nod and Dad would again take over the storytelling.

"So, Harv reaches over and turns my pencil upside down. *'What the hell do you think you are doing?'* I say to him: *'You want to ruin a perfectly good shirt with pencil marks?'*"

"Jack," explained our dad's boss, "*if this plane crashes, you could poke your eye out with that sharp point.* Am I right, kids?"

"Holy Hannah, Harv. Have you lost your ever-lovin' mind? Poke my eye out? If this plane is going down, WE are going down! Do you think I'd really care if they find me with a pencil sticking out of my eye!"

Mom would then steer the conversation to something else. Plane crashes. She didn't like to talk about that. Neither did I. It took all I had each week when Dad's plane was rising in the sky not to imagine it falling back down. Sometimes I had dreams about twisted metal and broken glass.

Every time Dad's boss came to our house, he'd remind us kids not to have sharp objects in our pockets, one time handing out plastic pocket protectors to all of us. Dad would shake his head at Harv's

39

twisted logic. "He's a smart man, but he has no common sense. And certainly none of our Kahmann sense!" Then Dad would throw back his head, like a hound dog howling at the moon, and laugh at his own pun until tears slid into his ears.

On Dad's return trip each Friday afternoon, Mom would get all dolled up in a pretty pleated dress, load us into the station wagon, turn off the radio, and drive us to the airport amidst a chorus of us singing the latest Broadway show tunes. *Showboat* was one of her favorites.

"*Fish gotta swim, birds gotta fly,*" Mom would sing. "*I gotta love one man till I die.*"

All of us: "*Can't help lovin' dat man of mine.*"

Then it was Eric and Andy's cue for the next verse: "*Tell me he's lazy, tell me he's slow. Tell me I'm crazy, maybe I know.*" Karl hit Andy upside the head and interjected: "Yeah, you are crazy!" but Mom just ignored him and kept on singing.

We all would chime in on the finale: "*He kin come home as late as can be. Home without him ain't no home to me ...*"

We'd all scream the ending, leaning out the back window of the station wagon. "*Can't help lovin' Dat. Man. Of. Mine!*" As if on cue, Dad would come running through the center doors of the airport, toss his suitcase to us in the backseat, take a deep, long drag of his *Camel* cigarette and motion for Mom to move over. He was in the driver's seat and all seemed right with the world.

Oklahoma! was Dad's new favorite musical, probably because there was a song about our own town, and we would serenade him home:

"*Everything's like a dream in Kansas City, It's better than a magic lantern show!*"

"Andy," asked Dad. "Why do you think they call Kansas City: the magic lantern show?"

"Cuz of all our streetlights!"

"Very good." Dad found a reason to turn every car ride into a history lesson, or at least a trivia session, even using song lyrics. He'd quiz us to see if we were paying attention.

"So, Karl, what about our streetlights?"

"We have more than any other city!"

"Per capita," Eric added. He was good in math.

Dad would boast that Kansas City was geographically the heart of the United States. "Every night her heart is lit up like a Christmas tree. Pilots notice. I've been on a plane when they announce the light show below!"

"Ja-a-ck," Mom would touch Dad's arm. "Enough with the quizzing."

"Well, it's something to be proud of, kids. And now it's immortalized in a musical!"

"Daddy, guess what happened when you were gone," one of us would report as we helped him unpack his suitcase. Treasures awaited us as we felt between the folds of Dad's clothes: monogrammed soaps and towels from the hotel, matchbooks from fancy restaurants, little bottles of booze from the airplane. We didn't get to drink the whiskey, but Dad would let us crack the seal on the little bottles and he'd gulp the contents one by one. Then we'd refill the miniatures with *Kool-Aid*, and pretend to have cocktail hour in our sandbox.

"Dad, isn't this stealing?" Eric would challenge, as we unfolded a fancy hotel towel.

"Hell, no," said Dad, grasping the thick thirsty cotton with a green stripe of lettering down the middle. "Why do you think they plaster the company name across it?"

"So people know it belongs to the ... *Waldorf-Astoria*?" Eric read.

"Don't be silly. It's the oldest gimmick in the book. They *want* people to take the towels—cheapest way to advertise—let the customer spread their identity all across the country."

Our clothesline became a colorful, waving billboard for some of the fanciest hotels in New York City.

41

CHAPTER 7
Hated Babysitters

1957 Kansas City

We hated having babysitters. Hated the word. We weren't babies. I don't know where our parents found the people they paid to look after us. Most of them treated us like infants, but mostly we hated Louise. She was an unhappy older woman who talked on the phone all the time and made us go to bed before our bedtime.

One Halloween Mom fell and broke her ankle while stepping up on a folding chair trying to kill a wasp. Dad was out of town and we came home from school to find Louise ironing our dishtowels and handkerchiefs. Mom never ironed dishtowels and it was my job to iron the handkerchiefs.

"The ambulance just took your mother away. Looks like she broke her leg. Hurry and get ready now." Louise had come to supervise our preparations for trick-or-treating that night. I was supposed to go as a witch and had practiced using Mom's red lipstick but the lipstick went with her to the hospital and the only thing I could find was red fingernail polish. I put that on my lips instead and Louise screamed at me.

"What a stupid child you are. Now look what I have to do."

With that she poured fingernail polish remover into a starched handkerchief and rubbed until my lips bled.

That night we came home with grocery bags full of candy. Louise let us pick out one piece and the next morning we awoke to find that she had put all of our bags in the garbage can outside and poured sand on top for good measure. We had worked hard for those bags, trudging through the dark to every house up and down the streets, keeping track of each other, worrying who was going to

43

pick the shortest straw and have to ring Johanna Johnson's house and have her scream at us. Sometimes we'd sneak home to change costumes and go around the neighborhood a second time. Then to sit on the living room floor surrounded by caramel apples and suckers and homemade cupcakes with sticky frosting and Lik-M-Aid and candy cigarettes, it was the payoff we had planned for and waited for since having to give up the ice cream-man-of-summer. And Louise took it all away.

When Dad came home from his business trip he was very mad and said he would never allow Louise in our house again. But that was before desperation for a sitter set in one night and everyone else was busy except Louise, who never was busy. Anyway, it was the beginning of Lent and we didn't have candy in the house, so I guess Dad thought it couldn't hurt to call her.

Then there was Linda who used to recite Bible verses. Linda lived on the next block and had just graduated from high school. She had been babysitting us for a couple years, but that summer we had her more often because she was saving money for Bible college in the fall. She could earn more at our house because Dad paid extra—even though we older kids did most of the work, making dinner, changing diapers, reading bedtime stories. Linda sat on the couch reading. If kids were fighting, she would slam her Bible shut, stand up and order us to pray. Each week she made us memorize a new Bible verse to recite to our parents, though it didn't seem to impress them.

Linda would come early on Saturdays so she could discuss the Bible with Dad, who loved to argue politics and religion.

"Close that Bible, Linda, and talk to me," Dad would say. "Tell me what you believe. Not what some old men wrote centuries ago." Linda would shudder when Dad talked like that. In her religion, the Bible was her manual.

"People hide behind the Bible," Dad would say. "Jesus didn't go around preaching from a book." He would challenge Linda with a trick question. "Tell me, Linda, who are God's chosen people, the Christians or the Jews?" She'd reach for her Bible and he'd snatch it away from her so she had to answer from her own knowledge.

"Well, the Christians, of course."

"Are you sure, Linda? Remember, Jesus was a Jew." It was a weekly game they played. Dad thought he was making progress. "That Linda is starting to think for herself."

After Mom and Dad left for dinner, Linda would pray feverishly. It was almost as if some cracks appeared in her thinking that she had to fill up. She'd pull out her Bible, stroke it lovingly, and make us memorize a new verse to recite to her before letting us have our dessert. That's how *she* played the game.

Even with all her Bible verses, Linda didn't have much patience with us. She got mad real easy and yelled a lot. When Eric would recite a Bible verse back at her, she really pitched a fit. "Blessed are the peacemakers, Linda, for they shall inherit the earth."

Linda always wore a dress because her religion wouldn't allow girls to wear pants. I often wondered if her religion knew you could see her underwear whenever she sat cross-legged on our couch.

As for the Saturday-night babysitter dilemma, with Linda moving away soon, Mom and Dad were running low on options, especially after the incident with our teenage cousins, the Twins. Jeannie and Joannie were our older cousins who came to take care of us the night Mom went into the hospital to have Kevin, Baby #7. Dad thought it would be okay, he said to Mom, but he seemed uneasy just the same.

Jeannie and Joannie taught us some things our parents would never have imagined. Jeannie would flip through the Kansas City telephone book and pick a number to call.

"This is a good one. Dial GL5-2345." Karl would dial it.

"Is your refrigerator running?" Joannie would say into the phone. Jeannie would lean into the receiver and shout. "Well, you better go catch it!" We'd scream with laughter. Our cousins were so clever; we never thought of those things on our own.

They weren't very good cooks, though. Joannie saw a pot of peeled potatoes in the sink that Mom had left behind. Joannie thought she knew how to make mashed potatoes. She covered the potatoes with milk and turned on the burner. Jeannie hollered at Joannie, "Uncle Jack said not to turn the stove on." The smell of gas was very strong. Karl struck a match, like we had seen Mom do many times, and the fire magically whooshed around the bottom of the pan. We were too young to convince Joannie she had it backwards. Who ever heard of boiling potatoes in milk?

Jeannie sided with us, but Joannie stuck her tongue out at her twin and turned back to the scorching pan. Paul, in his highchair, started crying. Eric gave him a bowl of fruit cocktail Mom had set out on the counter. It was to be our dessert. Paul eagerly ate whatever we put in front of him. I think he would have eaten Joannie's burnt potatoes, but they finally got thrown into the trash. The rest of us were happy to have cereal for supper.

Joannie wanted something else. She opened a cabinet we never, ever touched. Later, when Paul started vomiting and walking into walls, we knew we had to reach Dad at the hospital. We didn't tell him until he got home that we had poured Jack Daniel's and Beefeater's into Paul's fruit cocktail.

Dad never said a word to the Twins, not even when Aunt Helen came to pick them up, but the look he gave us cut to the bone. "You know better than that. I'm surprised at you." And then Johnny got left behind at the lake and it looked like we'd be stuck with old Louise for the summer.

CHAPTER 8
Miss Millie Bea

1957 Kansas City

We didn't always hate babysitters and a few were different from the rest, the ones that became part of the family. Carlene was a cool cowgirl who ran off with her rodeo boyfriend to a ranch in Wyoming. She would send newsy Christmas cards and promise to visit each summer, but we never saw her again.

During the week a lady came to us who called herself Black Mammy, and she told us to call her that, too. In Kansas City that was the norm, but Mom cringed and said where she came from, a lady who takes care of children should be called by her given name.

Millie Bea Jones wasn't really a babysitter, she was more than that. She came to help Mom during the week when Dad was traveling, and *helping Mom* meant keeping us kids occupied.

She was an older lady, like Louise, but she was nothing like Louise. She drove a shiny black Studebaker with whitewall tires and joked that she and her car were twins. She emerged from behind the wheel wearing a white hat and gloves, and a starched apron over a flowing black dress.

She agreed that we would call her Miss Millie Bea, or Miss Millie for short. Though whenever she drove up the driveway, she'd call out, "Here comes your black mammy!"

We would run down the front steps to meet her at the gate where she waited for us to calm Pepper's barking. She'd slowly take off her gloves, one finger at a time. When Pepper was quiet she'd nod her head and we'd unlatch the gate. Miss Millie Bea reached in her apron pocket and gave Pepper a treat. She'd bend down on one knee so she could be eye level to us. "Now, let's have a look-see."

If anyone had a bruise or scrape, she'd give you her focused attention. "Johnny, show me your bandage. Gotta see how those fingers are healing." Miss Millie would grab hold of the gate and one of our shoulders to help herself stand up straight. She would gather us all together for a hearty embrace and we'd follow her to the front steps. The top stoop is where she would sit and catch her breath.

I couldn't wait to show her the gravel burn on my wrist. "Miss Millie Bea, I fell off the swingset. The chain broke when I was going real high. I landed in the sandbox!" Miss Millie folded my arm in her apron and put her large warm hand over mine. She closed her eyes and mouthed a prayer. Miss Millie said the touch of a hand could heal, same as a doctor. You just had to believe. She gently traced the lines in my palm and whispered, "Why, do you know you have the mark of the *M*? I have one too. See?" Miss Millie pointed out how the lines in her palm crisscrossed to form a capital M. "Only a select few, PatsyGail, are lucky enough to possess the *M*."

One day I asked her: "Miss Millie Bea, why do they call you Black Mammy?"

"Honeychile, that wasn't the name I was born with; that's the name I earned. Same as how your momma earned hers, 'cuz of y'all."

"But why don't we just call you Mammy?"

"Cuz I'm not your mammy, I'm your black mammy."

"When I grow up, can I be a black mammy?"

Miss Millie Bea slowly shook her head and chuckled, "PatsyGail, you see this?" She held my arm securely next to hers. "See how it's different?" I could see how long and fat it was compared to mine. How it jiggled when she reached up into the cupboard. But I didn't want to tell her she was fat. Besides, she wasn't called Fat Mammy.

"Oh, child. Here," and Miss Millie turned her hand over and pinched the skin. "This. What color do you see?"

"Well, it's ... it's not black."

"I reckon you're right, child. Tell me what it looks like to you."

"I don't know ..."

Miss Millie would get cross with a plain answer. She kept at us until we came up with a more colorful one. She was always pointing out animals in storm clouds. A clump of weeds became a canopy of trees for the fairies living in-between the cracks in the sidewalks. That's why you never stepped on a crack.

"What do you see when you look at this old hand?"

" ... hot chocolate? ... Daddy's coffee, when he stirs in the cream?"

"That's more like it. And if we look at yours?"

"Freckles. I hate freckles."

"PatsyGail, you can do better than that. I would say your hand looks like the fairy folk sprinkled cinnamon all over you! How 'bout I call you Cinnamon Sugar?"

"And I'll call you Miss Cream."

"Ain't we a team, Cinnamon and Cream?"

"I wish my skin was like yours."

Miss Millie laughed until she had to wipe tears from her eyes. "Bless you, child, but you don't know what you're saying."

"... then the kids at school wouldn't call me Freckleface."

"They only say that because they wish they were touched by the fairy folk."

"I just wish my skin was one smooth color, like yours."

"Be careful what you wish for, maybe those spots'll all blend together one day."

"How I wish that would happen."

"Don't forget, child, you are blessed with the magic *M*."

"Just like you!"

"Yes, child, just like me."

I didn't always hate my freckles after that.

Another day I had another question: "Miss Millie Bea, can I ask you something else?"

"Shoot."

"Mom said you have your own family. Who takes care of your children when you take care of us?"

"Why, my chilren are all grown. My babies have babies of their own."

"Then ... that makes you a granny!"

"Honeychile, I been a granny a long time. My grandchildren are older'n you."

49

"You don't look like a granny."

Miss Millie Bea taught us the right way to play jacks, heaving her heavy breasts back and forth as she struggled to get herself situated down on the floor with us. She was so good at the game we only had to go chasing the little red ball once or twice. Then we'd all pull and push to help her get back up and her black face turned as red as the peppers she tossed into our tuna salad.

She started to teach me how to cook and didn't laugh like my brothers did when I tried to make pancakes for lunch. I stood on a chair at the kitchen counter and carefully stirred the bowl of batter. Miss Millie hollered out the ingredients from the living room couch where she sat folding towels.

"What do I put in next?" I thought she said three tablespoons of baking soda. Table Spoons are the big spoons. I knew that.

"Girl, what did you do?" she asked when she saw the batter bubbling and growing right out of the bowl.

And then she must have spotted the gold box of baking soda, because she reached high up in the cupboard, her black arm jiggling, and pulled down the round red can of baking powder.

"Oh, my lord. I believe you just invented somethin' new, child. My recipe takes three little teaspoons of this, the little spoon," she emphasized as she flicked her index finger on the side of the can causing it to ring a little.

"Well, let's see what happens when we put some heat under these bubbles. And, boys, you hush up," she said to my brothers at the table. "You'll eat these big, fat cakes because they'll make you grow tall."

Those pancakes, even with extra syrup on them, tasted like a dirty sponge, but my brothers quietly ate every last bite.

CHAPTER 9
Dad's Boss

1957 Kansas City

Our parents used a lot of witty phrases, favorite sayings, song lyrics even to make a statement, illustrate a lesson, teach us something.

≈

One of Mom's favorites: "This is how you acquire a beautiful singing voice: Eat the burnt toast!"

Dad would often say: "That's why they put erasers on pencils. Because people make mistakes."

Mom thought this song defined our family: "Keep your sunny side up. Hide the side that gets blue. Though you've had NINE SONS IN A ROW. Baseball teams make money you know!"

Another of Dad's favorites: "He ain't heavy, Father, he's my brother."

"Bored people are boring people," Mom would reply when we'd come to her with our late-summer complaints. "And so help me, Hannah, I'm not raising any boring kids! Now go outside and create something!"

"Ignorance of the law is no excuse."

Dad especially liked this one: "The boss may not always be right, but he's always the BOSS!"

≈

I remember the night I learned Miss Millie Bea's full name. Mom and Dad hosted an office party at our house for Dad's boss. It was to celebrate some big work event, "landing that Boston client" was what they called it. I was in the hallway when I overheard some things I shouldn't have. I learned a lot that night. Things I wanted to talk to Miss Millie about, but that would have to wait.

Us kids were to spend the evening in the new upstairs addition, but first we were formally introduced to the guests. Dad summoned us to line up in stair-step formation—tallest to smallest—as if we were an army platoon. Dad would shout: "State your name, rank, and serial number!"

"Karl Edward, #1, age 8."

"Patricia Gail, #2, age 7."

And so it would go. Our name was obvious: first and middle; rank was our birth order; and the serial number was our age. That's not really how the Army did it, but it always drew a laugh, which made Dad happy. Then we marched up to the Dormitory, which resembled an army barracks.

Dad had recently finished building this upstairs addition to our house. A dramatically wide staircase took you up to one enormous bedroom with single beds lined up on both sides with a walkway down the middle. Dad called it *Dormitory Kahmanns* and Karl made a sign with his woodburning set announcing the entrance at the top of the stairs. Sometimes I think Dad liked to relive his army days, the parts that involved his buddies. We never heard much about the bad parts of the war.

Dad put vertical bars on all the windows to keep the little ones from falling out. Dad's brother got killed as a child sitting in an upstairs window. The stick that propped up the window fell out and hit Joe on the head and he fell to the ground dead. Dad was determined to keep such a thing from happening to us.

Another fear Dad had was of fire. His grandmother burned her house down with a candle. And Dad's mother, our Granny, got a little crazy about fire after that and passed it along to her kids.

Every time Dad read about a house fire in the paper he would put us through an emergency fire drill where we tied bedsheets together, securing one end to a steel bar. Dad would call for Karl to demonstrate how to squeeze through the bars and shimmy down to the ground. But Karl was afraid of heights, so he managed to push Eric forward to do it.

In the Dormitory, it was comforting to have the beds so close together when the lights were out. Everyone had their own single bed, but in the morning you could often find Paul snuggled up next to Eric, or Johnny would be sleeping at the end of Andy's bed. Being the only girl I had my own room at the bottom of the stairs and I envied my brothers' nighttime togetherness.

At one end of the barracks was an area arranged as our second living room. It had a long couch, overstuffed chairs, a radio, phonograph, and later the first TV set in the neighborhood. Dad built a giant walk-in closet that housed all our clothes and linens. To get to it you had to climb a short flight of steps. It looked like a big black window in the wall. An ominous window. Dad temporarily jerry-rigged a hanging extension cord with a light socket at the end so we could see into the dark cavern, but due to Dad's fear of fire only he could turn the light on. Dad also promised to build a door, we hoped to keep the monsters contained, but he never got around to it. None of us kids ever went upstairs alone because of that dark window-closet. Not even Karl. He would bribe one of the younger kids to take the freshly-folded laundry up the stairs with him.

Dad had asked both Miss Millie Bea and Linda to come and help with the party preparations. Miss Millie and I spent the afternoon in the kitchen where she produced some of the most amazing little foods. I ached to be in the kitchen with her now. Instead, my brothers and I took turns playing detective at the top of the stairs and keeping track of the adults and devising a plan to get us some of that food.

Andy's job was to sneak through Mom and Dad's bedroom to the kitchen. Dad's latest remodeling project had been to build a set of French doors that opened from their bedroom onto the screened-in back porch. The porch stretched along the entire back of the house, with an entrance to the kitchen at the far end. This formed a circle inside the house that allowed us to sneak into the kitchen. It also made hide-and-seek a much more acceptable indoor game.

Eric and Karl kept Linda occupied by asking Bible questions. "Linda, what does 'beget' mean?" I kept guard at the bottom of the staircase for any sign of Andy. Miss Millie had a soft spot for Andy and he could get her to supply us with some of her concoctions. But we didn't want him to linger and risk getting caught or to hog all the food.

The crowd began to spill into the hallway, close to where I was keeping guard. I heard something that made me take notice—my name. Creeping closer, I pressed myself up against the door to the basement, which was right next to the bathroom. Mom and Mrs. Ringheim were standing close by. Mom had her back to me.

"... yes, and Mildred is the lady who has been teaching Patsy. She's been a godsend. When Jack's on the road, I don't know what I would do without her. She's ..."

Just then Dad's boss came out of the bathroom and bumped his wife's elbow, spilling her drink all over. Mom tried to reach into the bathroom for a towel, but Mr. Ringheim grabbed her shoulder and blocked the doorway.

"Della," he stated loudly. "Let me straighten you out right now. Looks like you Yankees need an education in our Kansas City ways. That woman in the kitchen you just called a lady. Make no mistake, she is no lady. You understand? She's a colored."

The clinking and clanking of glasses and chattering voices had stopped. Without hesitation our mother did something so startling it took my breath away. She raised her voice to a guest, to Dad's boss!

"Harv," Mom said loudly as she flicked his hand off her shoulder. "Any woman who takes care of my children is a lady. Understand? Make no mistake, Mildred Beatrice Jones is a lady. You, and everyone else in my home will treat her as such. Now, you will excuse me." Mom turned away, ignoring the spilled drink and headed for her bedroom.

I slinked back to the stairway where Andy appeared with a plate of cookies that no longer looked appealing.

My throat felt tight, and my stomach quivered. Mildred Beatrice Jones. What a big name!

I didn't want to spy on any more adults. I wanted to run and find Miss Millie Bea in the kitchen, but the stairway held me. There was too much to think about.

I needed to tell Karl and Eric what I had overheard. This didn't add up. We liked Mr. Ringheim. He seemed genuinely interested in us kids, even when no one was looking. He asked questions more engaging than: "What grade are you in?" He carried silver dollars in his pockets and would toss us one for every new joke we told.

Something big had happened in the hallway and I didn't know what to make of it. I needed Mom.

From my place on the stairs, I could hear her whispering in the bedroom. I started to go to her, but a commotion coming from the living room caught my eye. Mrs. Ringheim was staggering down the hallway, bumping into walls, spilling a fresh drink. I used to think she was so pretty with her loud bracelets and bright red lipstick. But now she looked like Paul after he ate that fruit cocktail.

Suddenly, Mrs. Ringheim had her hand on the door. But it was the wrong door! "No, that's not the bathroom!" I screamed, but the warning came too late. She had already opened the door and stepped in where there was no floor, only steps leading down to the concrete basement. She didn't scream or anything. I only heard a loud thud.

"Mom!" I didn't want to be the first one to find her. Mom ran to the basement door.

"Oh, my God."

I peered around the doorframe and saw Mrs. Ringheim lying on a mountain of our dirty clothes, including wet diapers, which we always threw down the stairs. Eric and Andy were supposed to have put those clothes in the washing machine that afternoon. Oh, they were going to be in trouble.

"Where's the goddamn toilet? And my drink? Someone keeps spilling my drink." Mrs. Ringheim stood up like she did this sort of thing every day.

Mom helped her up the stairs, pulling a wet diaper off Mrs. Ringheim's back. Dad stood beside me shaking his head. "Damndest thing I ever saw. I can't believe she didn't break her neck."

Eric and Andy probably weren't getting in trouble. That pile of dirty clothes had saved a life.

"Harv, I'm sorry," Dad said. "These doors all look alike when they're closed. I've been meaning to do something about that."

Mr. Ringheim laughed at his wife. It didn't seem to bother him that she fell down the stairs. The next day Dad built a covering on the staircase. After that when you opened the door from the hallway, you had to open another door built into the floor. It was like opening the cellar door in *The Wizard of Oz*. I couldn't wait to show Miss Millie Bea our entrance to Dorothy's farm. Soon after that night I awoke from a dream and heard Miss Millie's voice: "PatsyGail." I opened my eyes and I saw her on the stairs. But it was mom who called to us: "Time to get up, kids. Gotta get Dad to the airport." Miss Millie usually came to stay when Dad was on the road, but when we got back from the airport, her shiny Studebaker wasn't sitting in the driveway. Instead, the phone was ringing and it was one of her sons calling to tell us something awful.

Miss Millie Bea had died in her sleep. She was the first person we knew who had died.

We didn't go to her funeral. Dad wasn't home to drive us to that part of town. But Mom felt the need to visit the family and bring flowers. "Don't tell your father," Mom said. "Is that clear?"

"Yes, Mom." Only Karl, Eric and I got to drive with her across town to Miss Millie's house.

Mom didn't have to tell us twice. Something about this car trip felt like an important mission. The neighbor lady had come to watch the rest of the kids. Mom didn't even tell *her* the truth of where we were going.

Highway 71, the main thoroughfare slicing Kansas City down the middle, narrowed when it left downtown. Mom turned off on a side street and stopped at an old gas station to double-check her written directions. The streets were crowded with parked cars on both sides, allowing only one lane for two-way traffic. Luckily, we didn't meet another car. Block after block Mom stared straight ahead. Eric was charged with clocking the house numbers.

"It's the next block, Mom." Many houses fit on each street, built close together, all looking the same, with front porches and several pairs of eyes staring at us.

"That's it, Mom," shouted Karl at last. "That's the one."

"Where are we going to park?" asked Eric.

"There's Miss Millie Bea!" I screamed.

A large woman ran down the front steps. I never saw Miss Millie run before.

"Ma'am, drive right up on the lawn here. Boys, open up a space for the lady."

Two parked cars began to move, one forward, one back, opening up a space for us, an impossibly small space, that allowed Mom to maneuver our station wagon up onto the grass. We had never seen her drive like that before. I couldn't take my eyes off of Miss Millie Bea. I thought she was dead.

"Mrs. Kahmann, how do you do? My mother would have been so pleased. She loved y'all's kids. This must be PatsyGail. How do you do, missy? My momma sure talked about y'all."

"Your mother had wages due her and I wanted to bring them myself. I want to tell you in person how sorry I am for your loss. She was very dear to me and my children."

"My mother was very fond of your family. She told us many lovely stories. Thank you for being so kind."

We drove home in silence. Mom never had to say another word about keeping this secret from Dad. We never even talked about it amongst ourselves. It was all too mysterious, the unfamiliar streets, the way Mom drove that day, this whole dying thing. *Where did Miss Millie Bea go?*

Months later Karl, Eric and I found ourselves driving with Dad to his company's warehouse near downtown Kansas City. On the way home a wrong turn had us heading south instead of north. The first bleak gas station we came to Dad pulled in to turn around. Karl looked over at me and shook his head slightly. We recognized it as the turnoff to Miss Millie's street. Dad pulled up close to the station and told us to roll up the windows and lock the doors while he ran in for a pack of cigarettes. He returned in mere seconds with a frosty bottle of Grape Nehi for us to share. "Your mother doesn't need to know about this shortcut."

Miss Millie Bea was on my mind all the way home. Sometimes I thought I could hear her calling to me: *"PatsyGail. Come here, chile."* But it scared me. I quit hanging out in the kitchen. Cooking no longer held my interest. She had promised to be my teacher and it just wasn't the same. Whenever she'd start to fade from my mind, I'd check the *M* on my hand. It made me think of her. I just couldn't believe Miss Millie, our black mammy, was never coming back. We missed her so. None of the string of babysitters after her quite measured up.

That is, until Jimmy Maines came into our life.

CHAPTER 10
The Bowling Boy

1957 Kansas City

We had a few secrets to keep that summer, my brothers and me. Not bad secrets, but protective ones. Mom said people don't always tell the whole truth and that's why they might feel the need to keep a secret. Dad called it a Sin of Omission if you didn't tell the whole truth, but Mom disagreed. "Sometimes people are trying to protect something or someone."

I was seven in 1957 the first time I remember her saying that. Karl was a year older than I and Eric a year younger, and together we became a trio of experts in keeping things under wraps.

Jimmy Maines was the Keeper of a Secret. We became his unwitting Helpers. It was a big secret, an important one. If you could weigh it Jimmy said it weighed more than a bowling ball. We felt its heft completely.

If anyone asked us any questions, we would have to lie. Eric said this would be a Gentle Lie, so we would not get in trouble. Gentle Lies, according to Mom, were the kind that didn't hurt anyone, they protected someone. For example, you tell Granny she looks lovely in her new hat, even though she doesn't. You tell the neighbor her baby is cute, though he looks like an old man.

"Anyway," Karl said, "a secret is not a lie because you're not talking out loud. You're keeping it to yourself." It felt important to be the Helpers to Jimmy's secret.

Jimmy Maines came to us like a gift from the heavens, a golden-tanned giant of a high school kid. He came at just the right time, when we were bored with summer and still sad about Miss Millie. He had been hired a few times to "spend time" with us, as he called it. His parents were church friends with Mom and Dad, but Jimmy was too busy to be a regular.

Dad offered to pay him more than he was making as a lifeguard, so that's how we came to have the coolest babysitter a kid could ever imagine. All our friends thought so too. No one else had a guy as their babysitter, let alone one with his own hotrod. Jimmy didn't like to be called a babysitter. "You're not babies and I'm not sitting! You can say I'm a coach."

He came to play games with us, not to bark orders or hurry us off to bed so he could eat popcorn and talk on the phone. He came to take us places with him. Sometimes we would go to Jimmy's house where he let us ride his family's go-carts. We got to help him polish his hotrod that he was planning to race in the fall. He called it *Jimmy's Jalopy*. We loved it when he would try to return the money Dad gave him for his time. And we loved it more when Dad insisted that he keep it.

Jimmy wouldn't be able to start as our coach until he had found a replacement lifeguard. We had been waiting all week for him. We finally got the news he'd be coming on Monday. But on Saturday, our parents had a wedding to go to and we were hoping Jimmy could start sooner. Mom reminded us that Jimmy was busy. It was looking like we would have to have Louise, who was never busy. All week we prayed that God would intervene and make Jimmy our babysitter/coach instead.

By Thursday we decided we would have to take matters into our own hands. "Let's say the rosary, maybe that'll help," suggested Eric.

Karl, since he was the oldest and an altar boy, led us in prayer. "Dear God." As we knelt down beside our beds, Karl continued. "We offer up this rosary so You will let Jimmy Maines come and be with us on Saturday instead of Louise. Hail Mary, full of Grace, the Lord is with thee. Blessedartthouamongwomen and Blessedisthefruitof thywomb, Jesus."

"HolyMary," the rest of us would rush to continue, "Motherof-God, prayforussinners nowandatthehourofourdeath,amen."

We said this prayer *fifty* times that night to finish the rosary. On Friday morning I heard Mom on the phone. "Louise is in the hospital? It's her gallbladder, you say?" She turned to Dad. I turned and ran up the wide hallway steps, shaking from the power we had just been granted. Could a rosary said by a bunch of kids cause a woman's gallbladder to rise up and put her in the hospital? I stopped before the last step when I heard Mom.

"I'll have to call Jimmy. He said if we were desperate he would change his plans."

My brothers joined me on the stairway. "Jimmy's coming early!" we screamed. One thing was obvious, Jimmy was meant to be with us.

We played school on the front porch steps while waiting for Jimmy Maines to come. Six of us waited on the steps for him, each of us struggling to be the first to see him drive up in his polished jalopy.

Kevin lay in the baby buggy beside the station wagon. He was only a few months old and would be going with Mom and Dad to a wedding. Mom was still nursing Kevin, so he couldn't be left with us. Dad was not eager to go to this wedding. "I have to be a pallbearer for Harv's cousin," Dad joked.

"Jack, don't be facetious. We are not going to a funeral, kids." Dad was a groomsman for a relative of Dad's boss. The guy had been married before. Divorce wasn't allowed in our religion, but Dad couldn't say No to his boss, who was not Catholic. And that—not being Catholic—was another problem. Sister Rose Dorothy told us that if you weren't Catholic, you weren't allowed in heaven. That made me sad to think all the kids in our neighborhood and our Dad's boss were doomed. Sister said it's just easier not to become friends with those people, unless you planned to convert them.

Jimmy was late so while Dad paced beside the baby buggy and smoked another *Camel*, we continued our game of "school." Karl got to be the teacher because he was the oldest. He was eight years old. I was seven, Eric was six, Andy four, Johnny three, and Paul was almost two. Karl would hide a stone in one hand behind his back and one-by-one we picked which hand held the stone. When you picked the right one, he nodded, and you got to move up a step. The first one to the top got to be Teacher. When Karl played, no one ever graduated to the next step. But when Jimmy came, *that* was a different game.

He'd let Karl get almost to the top and then, magically, Karl stayed put while the rest of us passed him by.

"He's here! He's here!" shouted Eric and we all scrambled down the steps and ran to his green Jeep, and pulled him out of the car towards the house. "Play school with us, Jimmy. You be Teacher," we begged. Jimmy seemed more excited than ever to see us. We could tell because he stuttered more when he was excited. He stuttered more around adults, too, not so much with us. Jimmy looked around and counted heads and talked to Mom and Dad about when they were due back.

"Goo..goo..good-bye, Mr. and Mrs. Ka..Ka..Kahmann. Don't w..w..worry about a th..th..th..th..thing." Jimmy hollered above Pepper's frantic barking.

Jimmy picked up the stone from our game of school and tossed it up in the air. We could tell he was thinking about something, planning something. He squinted his eyes and bit his lips and kept tossing the stone up in the air catching it, twisting it around the palm of his hand, sometimes switching it to the other hand and tossing it back up in the air.

"How would y'all li..li..like to go roller skating?" he asked. Wow, our other babysitters never thought of that.

"I'll go get the clamp-ons," I said as I ran up the steps. But Jimmy stopped me.

"Not that kind of skating. At a ro..ro..roller rink. Inside. Antioch Shopping Center has a new one that I wa..wa..want to take you to."

"Jimmy, you're the best," said Karl as we piled into his old green jalopy. Karl got to sit up front with Paul in the middle. Eric and Andy and Johnny and I all sat in the back hardly believing we could be going on such an adventure. I got to sit right behind Jimmy while he was driving and I tried to keep my shoes from hitting his bowling ball on the floor. But it was hard.

A new shopping center had opened in North Kansas City about five miles from our house. It was called Antioch and was something truly wonderful. An indoor shopping center. I had been there a couple of times with Mom but the others hadn't. There were stores all over connected to each other and a place where you could jump on trampolines as high as you could go. They were built right into the ground, so you didn't have to climb up on them. Just jump to your heart's content for 25 cents an hour. Downstairs there was an indoor roller skating rink where you could rent real wooden-wheeled roller skates that laced up and stayed on your feet, not like the clamp-on ones that would come undone just as the ride was getting good.

Jimmy was excitedly pointing to a new bowling alley across the street from the shopping center.

"Since y'all like to skate so much I was wo..wo..wondering if you mind if I run across to the bowling alley for a f..f..few minutes. I was supposed to talk to someone there today."

Of course, we said, that would be fine and Jimmy walked us down the cement steps leading to the roller skating rink, which was under the shopping center. He paid for all our skates, except for Paul who was too small. We told Jimmy not to worry, we would take turns holding him in our arms as we whirled around the wooden circle. Jimmy seemed anxious. He kept walking away and then coming back. He gave Karl a couple dollars.

"Don't wo..wo..worry, I'll be r..r..r..r..right back."

But he didn't come right back.

Paul needed his diaper changed. I had only brought one. Johnny was crying and pulling on my hand.

"I want to go home. Now."

Karl came from the counter with a hot dog and a root beer with three straws. He ripped the hot dog into pieces and gave one to Andy, Johnny, and Paul, who had filled up on candy earlier. That's what we thought the money had been for. We didn't know it was going to be supper.

I looked around for Eric but couldn't see him in the crowd of skaters. "Karl, you have to go look for him. We're supposed to stick together." Just then Eric came through the front door. "Where've you been?" demanded Karl.

"I went to see if I could find his car. But I can't tell for sure if the jalopy's over there."

"From now on we stick together." Karl decided we should do our Sound-Off. Somehow it felt comforting.

"Patsy."
"Here."
"Eric."
"Here."
"Andy."
"I'm here and I'm hungry."
"Johnny."
"Here."
"Paul."

Paul, leaning beside me on the bench, was asleep. We knew we couldn't stay in the roller rink much longer. People were starting to look at us funny. It was decided we should wait for Jimmy outside on the concrete steps. Eric came back from returning our skates with a big grin on his face. I thought he had found Jimmy.

"Look, I got two dollars and fifty cents." Dad always called Eric *Moneybags*.

"What did you do, Eric?"

"It's what you call a deposit. It belongs to Jimmy, but I don't think he'd mind if we got some more hot dogs."

We sent Eric to the counter and told him to meet us on the steps outside. I lifted up Paul and his head fell on my shoulder. Karl took Johnny's hand. "We have to hold hands now. Andy, take Johnny's other hand." We felt safer on the steps. No one peering at us over a counter, or asking where we were from, or where our Mom and Dad were. My arms began to quiver and my legs were wet from holding Paul but I didn't want to set him down and have him wake up. Karl decided we should play school to pass the time and everybody started searching for a rock. I looked up to see a huge shadow on the top of the stairway.

"Jimmy!"

He had a big bulky object in his hand and he bounded down the steps three at a time. Jimmy sat down beside Paul and me, trying to catch his breath.

"I am so, so sorry. I didn't mean to be gone so long. I will owe y'all for the rest of my li..li..life for today."

He reached over and grabbed as many of us as he could get his arms around and hugged us and squeezed us and kept saying how sorry he was.

"I have to tell y'all something and this is very special because I can only tell YOU. Nobody else in the whole world can I tell."

And then Jimmy began to explain to us about bowling and how he was the captain of his high school team. About the new Antioch Bowling Alley and how they were having their Grand Opening. About how he had been given a free game when he walked in the door. He was just going to look around. Check it out. "I just love the game, y'all." Next to his jalopy, Jimmy's prized possession was his very own bowling ball.

"Today, y'all. You're not going to believe this!" Jimmy stood up and pointed to his trophy.

"I bowled a perfect game!"

We could tell by Jimmy's smile that was something huge. Karl knew what it meant. "Wow, Jimmy, that's like pitching a no-hitter."

"Or hitting a hole-in-one," said Eric.

"Are you crazy, Eric? A hole-in-one is mostly luck. This is more like a no-hitter. Right, Jimmy?"

"What do you know, Karl?"

"I know more'n you."

"Hey, guys, it doesn't matter. All I know is, it may never happen again. I ff..ff..ffeel so bad for y'all having to wait, but they wouldn't let me go. It's the first perfect game at that bowling alley. On opening day! People were cheering and taking pictures. The newspaper interviewed me for a story. I tried, to leave y'all, but they wouldn't let me go."

And then Jimmy started crying. "I can't even tell my folks. You know they'd k..k..kill me if they knew I had left you kids. Do you know what this means? Y'all are the only ones I can ever tell."

"But, Jimmy, if it's in the papers, your Mom and Dad'll know," Karl said.

"That's no problem. I'm their paperboy. I got it figured out. I'll hide this trophy in my car. But you gotta see this."

He held up the game sheet and it was filled with big furious black marks all the way across the page.

We knew what those marks meant. One time when Jimmy had taken some of us for a ride in his convertible we stopped at a bowling alley. He showed us how the game was played and taught us how to keep score. Karl could just barely swing the heavy ball past his body and bring it back and drop it with a big thud on the wooden lane. The finger holes were too far apart for me, so Jimmy showed me how to place the ball on the foul line and push with all my might. We willed that wobbling ball down the lane towards the pins.

When it was Jimmy's turn he made it seem so smooth as he stood there poised to go. He wasn't a kid who stuttered as he brought the ball to his chin. He would crouch his shoulders just so and slightly bend his body forward. And he would pause. Suddenly, before you could breathe, he and the ball would connect with the lane, and those pins didn't stand a chance.

"Jimmy, what about our Mom and Dad?" I asked. Jimmy looked like someone had slapped him. "Don't worry," said Karl, "I'll take care of the newspaper." I better get y'all b..b..back home. But first we got something to do. You gotta celebrate with me." With that Jimmy dried his eyes and stood up. He seemed so tall and big standing up.

And then he started singing his favorite song: *"Ain't nothin' but a hound dog. Cryin' all the time."*

Jimmy never stuttered when he sang. We started singing too and it helped us forget about the afternoon hours. *"Well, you ain't never caught a rabbit. And you ain't no friend of mine."*

Jimmy took Paul from my arms and held him high in the sky. We passed his trophy around and took turns carrying it back to the car, singing as we went. Before he took us home Jimmy stopped at an ice cream parlor where he handed a hundred-dollar bill to the waitress to pay for everything.

"It's a C..C..C-note," Jimmy explained. "That's my winnings."

Daylight was dwindling by the time Jimmy's Jalopy with six tired kids turned onto 74th Street Northeast. As we got to the top of the hill, we could hear Pepper's barking. Usually Jimmy would help us try to sneak up on Pepper. He would shut off the car at the bottom of the hill while we walked up as quietly as we could but it didn't matter. Somehow Pepper always knew when we were coming home. Jimmy would rev up his jalopy, zoom up the hill after us and squeal into our driveway. This night we weren't surprised when Jimmy didn't stop and instead drove us carefully up the hill.

I think he was relieved that we got home before Mom and Dad. I was glad it was too late for Saturday-night baths. Slowly we all climbed up the wide stairway to the Dormitory. Jimmy followed, walking up and down between the beds, making sure everyone was tucked in. He stopped at the landing to turn off the light, but turned back and suddenly sat down at the top of the stairs. "I feel like there's something sitting on my chest, y'all."

"It'll be okay," said Karl, tossing off his covers and going to him. Jimmy shook his head. "I knew it was wrong when I was knocking those pins down. I just couldn't stop it." One by one we all gathered around Jimmy. He didn't say anything for the longest time. "If you ever want to look at my trophy, y'all just sa..sa..say the word. Okay? It'll be hiding in the trunk of my car."

"Don't worry, Jimmy," said Eric, patting him on the shoulder. "You're secret's safe with us." And then we all put one hand on top of another hand on top of another, all the way to the top of Jimmy's trophy as a sign that we were in this together.

"Jimmy, you're the best," said Eric, "way better'n Louise."

CHAPTER 11
Gentle Lies

1957 Kansas City

"Can you bowl with this bowl?" Johnny asked as he leaned over his oatmeal the next morning. Karl looked across the table at me and I looked over at Eric and Eric kicked Johnny under the table.

"Shut up," I whispered in my sternest and quietest voice.

Dad was just coming in the front door. He had been to early Mass and he was carrying the *Kansas City Star* in his hand. Mom flipped pancakes on the long, black pan for those who didn't want cereal. Dad began to snap open the paper. Karl winked at me. I knew he had hidden the sports section.

"Della, call the *Star* tomorrow and ask them why we didn't get the Sports section. And tell them they better not charge for today. Nothing older than yesterday's news."

All of a sudden Pepper started barking frantically and I saw a silver car go slowly by the front of the house. Pepper kept barking. That meant somebody was coming up the driveway.

Karl, Eric, and I ran to the front door. Mr. Maines was just getting out of his car. Jimmy stepped out of the back seat of the silver car and stood behind his father. He didn't look as big as yesterday. Jimmy followed his parents through the gate and towards our front steps. He kept his eyes on the ground. Mom came out to the front stoop.

"Florence, it's so good to see you." Mom and Mrs. Maines were good friends from church.

Dad slapped Mr. Maines on the back, "Hey, Kenny, I didn't see you in early Mass this morning. Must've had a late one last night."

Mrs. Maines pulled back from Mom's hug. "Jimmy has something he wants to talk to you about."

Jimmy started to talk but his stuttering was worse than ever. Mr. and Mrs. Maines never would talk for Jimmy, allowing him to take as long as it took. But he got so jumbled no one, but us kids, could understand him. "Mr. Ka..Ka..Ka..Kaha..ma..ma..man. Mrs. Ka..ka.. ka..Mrs ..."

Mr. Maines couldn't hold back, "Jimmy bowled a 300 game. Y'all didn't see it in the paper?"

Dad got so excited, slapping Jimmy on the back. Jimmy was trying not to smile, trying not to get caught up in the excitement of Dad's exuberance.

"Haven't had a chance to read the paper."

"It happened yesterday," Mrs. Maines explained. "A reporter called to verify that our son was truly 16 years old. They couldn't believe it. They congratulated me on his becoming the youngest person in Kansas City to bowl a perfect game. The headline called our Jimmy: *The Bowling Boy Wonder*."

"The first perfect game," added Mr. Maines. "The new bowling alley got their first perfect game. Unexpected publicity for that!"

"Wow, Jimmy. Fantastic. I'm so proud of you." And that's when Jimmy began to cry. Mom and Dad looked puzzled. Mr. and Mrs. Maines looked at each other. We were fidgeting.

"Della. Jack." Mrs. Maines looked from Mom to Dad. "This happened yesterday. When Jimmy was supposed to be watching your children."

Everything around us sort of stopped. No one spoke. Luckily Kevin cried out from his highchair in the kitchen and we all followed Mom through the front door. Dad told everybody to sit down in the living room. "Kenny, Florence, how about some coffee? Jimmy, do you want some coffee?"

"N..n..no, sir." Jimmy shook his head and wiped his eyes.

Mom came back into the living room with a certain kind of smile on her face. Dad was doing his best to keep the silence from catching up on us again.

"I don't think I want to know the details. Except. How long did you leave the kids alone here?"

Silence again.

"Oh, it doesn't matter now. They're obviously all right. They're pretty good about taking care of each other."

Karl piped in with a Gentle Lie. "We weren't alone very long, Dad. We were just fine."

But Mr. Maines wouldn't let it rest.

"The kids weren't alone *here*, Jack. He took them to the roller rink across from the new bowling alley."

Eric told Gentle Lie #2: "We didn't skate very long. It was fun. Jimmy was back just like that." Eric slapped his hands together because he couldn't snap his fingers.

I stood close to Paul, and Karl inched over to Johnny ready to put a hand to his mouth just in case he started to say something different.

Dad only hesitated for a second. He sucked in his breath and said, "Hey, wasn't a very smart thing to do, Jimmy ole boy, but you know what? I think you already got your punishment."

"It ju..ju..just happened so fast, Mr. Kahmann."

"Twelve strikes in a row. You bring that trophy over for me to see sometime."

"Yes, sir."

"I do need to know something, Jimmy. Do you realize what you did with the kids was wrong?"

Jimmy nodded his head. "It would never happen again, sir, I promise. You'll see."

"Congratulations, Jimmy," Mom said with her tight smile as they stood up. Jimmy left our house smiling. Everything was fine. But Mom didn't smile after they were gone and sent the youngest outside to play.

Karl, Eric and I sat on the couch waiting for the punishment we knew was coming.

"What possessed you to keep that a secret?" Dad asked, but didn't wait for an answer. "I want a play-by-play of everything you did while Jimmy was at the bowling alley."

We might have committed a Sin of Omission after we replayed the afternoon at the Antioch Roller Rink. We dodged Mom's repeated question about how long we were left alone. We emphasized how we didn't talk to strangers or let anyone out of our sight, but Dad was still not appeased. "How in the world did you think we wouldn't find out? Judas H Priest! What were you thinking?"

"Ja-a-ck," Mom interjected. "We should thank these three for keeping the others safe. You deserve a lot of credit for watching out for each other."

"We only did what we knew we were supposed to," Karl volunteered.

"Yeah, it wasn't that bad. Really," added Eric. "Everybody behaved."

"Please, don't be mad at Jimmy," I begged. "He needs us. He doesn't hardly stutter when he's around us. Please give him another chance."

"We'll think about it" was all Mom would say.

"Is it too early to mix up a martini?" Dad asked Mom.

Cascone's restaurant didn't see the Kahmanns on their Saturday night date nights for awhile. For a long while, it seemed. When the neighborhood card parties started in the fall we endured a string of forgettable babysitters, never Jimmy. As gracious as Mom tried to be about his bowling success, she let us know that Jimmy had lost his job as a Kahmann babysitter.

From time to time we would see Jimmy in church and after Mass we'd run to him. He was never too cool to stop and gather us around and bear hug us like we were still something to him.

We stopped pleading with Mom and Dad to hire Jimmy again. Instead we tried to use logic to show them we didn't need an outsider to take care of us.

"Dad, what about the day Jimmy left us? We took good care of each other. We did the Sound-Off. Paul's diaper got changed. No one went hungry."

"Mom, we kept each other safe. We can do a better job than Louise or Linda. Please let us prove it."

Then one Saturday in late autumn we were summoned to Dad's office in the basement. A card party at the Baxter's next door became an opening.

"Karl and Patsy, you will be in charge tonight. Eric is the backup. If you two don't agree on something, Eric will have the deciding vote. Is that clear? I don't expect you to disappoint us. We'll be next door at the Baxter's playing cards."

Our job was to put the kids to bed. No baths allowed. Everyone went upstairs at bedtime without too many delays. Karl and I walked up and down between the beds making sure everyone was tucked in. We could hear Pepper pacing and whining below. I stopped and looked out of a window and saw Mom and Dad walking up the driveway arm in arm. Their card party must have ended early.

Then Karl remembered something. "Hey, you guys. Hit the floor." We had forgotten our nightly prayers. Everyone knelt beside a bed. Karl led us from Dad's usual place at the top of the stairs. I knelt beside Kevin's crib. "*Day Is Done,*" he began to sing.

"*Gone the sun,*" we joined in. "*From the lakes. From the hills. From the sky.*"

And then, as we did every night, we stopped our singing and began to pray.

"God bless Mommy. God bless Daddy. God bless KarlPatsy EricAndy..."

"Stop it, Karl, we can't rush it like that," Eric said.

"Okay. God bless Karl. God bless Patsy. God bless Eric. God bless Andy. God bless Johnny. God bless Paul. God bless Kevin. God bless everybody in the wholewideworldAmen."

"Don't forget Jimmy Maines," someone added.

"And what about Miss Millie? We can't forget her."

"God bless Miss Millie Bea and The Bowling Boy!"

As we began to sing again we heard Mom and Dad join in from the bottom of the stairs, their voices rising up to the top of the house, "*All is well. Safely rest. God is nigh.*"

The final notes lingered awhile, holding us all together.

After that summer we only saw Jimmy Maines a couple times. He never took care of us again; we never got to ride in his old jalopy.

He went away to college and we moved away from Kansas City. But we kept praying for him like he belonged to us. Later we would hear he died of an unnamed illness. He never married. He never had children. He never became a champion bowler. But for that one summer he had us kids and we had the coolest coach. And together we shared the glory of his one perfect game.

The future has
an ancient heart.
— **Carlos Levi**

CHAPTER 12
Ten Houses

Winter, 1964 Granite Falls, Minnesota
The In-Between Time

Where is my baby sister?

I don't remember dreaming during those nights we were in foster care. I do remember waking up at 3 a.m., out of breath, my hands tingling. Before the accident Beth had taken to crawling out of her crib and finding her way to my bed. I'd change her wet diaper and we'd snuggle till morning. Who was watching over her as she awoke in an unfamiliar bed in the middle of the night?

Ten couples came forward that day and opened their homes—for how long no one knew. Their spontaneous generosity was honorable and decent and good.

But. It's complicated—what happened to us after we were taken away. How do I convey what really happened to some of us in some of the homes? Telling the hard truth seems ungracious, but gentle lies would not be honest. One thing is clear—not everyone is emotionally equipped to handle other people's kids, let alone able to deal with the tears and trauma of torn-apart kids.

I overheard a teacher saying that ten families got to be heroes for taking in one or two of "those Kahmann kids." The heroes could have been the childless couple who offered to move in to our house to keep us together, but Father Buckley wouldn't hear of it.

On that Wednesday afternoon, the day after the accident, I walked from school to the Grant house. Their kitchen lights were so bright it hurt my eyes. I noticed my pajamas folded neatly on top of the counter. "Here, Patty, I fixed this for you," and Mrs. Grant unfolded my pajama bottoms and pointed to a pearly white button.

"My name is not Patty."

"Well, I replaced that safety pin on your pajamas. I was expecting a Thank You." Mrs. Grant turned to Mr. Grant who had just walked in. "I can't imagine a mother letting her child go to bed with a pin in her pajamas. That's dangerous."

"What about your baby's diaper?" I said loudly. "It's called a *safety* pin." How dare this woman say anything against my mother? "And my name is not Patty. It's Patsy. My mom named me after Patsy Cline."

Mr. Grant grabbed the kitchen counter, "You cannot talk to my wife that way, young lady."

I don't know what came over me. Suddenly I became a kid who talked back to adults. What did I have to lose by using my words. When your mom is dying, what does anything matter?

The next day my classmate Connie told me I'd be going home to stay with her family. They wouldn't let me go back to get my things or to tell my brother Johnny. I wasn't sorry to leave that woman and her husband behind, but I hated that Johnny had to stay there and I couldn't explain to him why they were sending me away without a goodbye.

Later I'd feel bad about my behavior, but never enough to apologize, even though Father Buckley insisted I should.

Over the coming days I tried to fill in the blanks on my list of where my brothers and sisters were.

This much I knew:

I knew Eric was safe with the Wengerts. Karl was safe with the Rileys. John was ... not really safe but I knew where he was. That haunts me still, knowing what he was going through.

My list of temporary houses:
    Karl   the Rileys
    Patsy   the Grants
    Eric   the Wengerts
    Andy   ??
    John   the other Grants
    Paul   ??
    Kevin ??

Katy ??
Karen ??
Phillip ??
Jimmy ??
Beth ??

I had never felt so unmoored. Our parents were in a hospital 70 miles from home.

And what was home?

I pictured our farmhouse. Empty. It had never been silent since the day we moved in, except the few Sunday mornings we all went to church together—taking up two pews for all 14 of us. Because we rode to church in a pickup truck we could only attend Mass as a complete family during good weather.

On the days we went to church as a family, the house was never truly empty. Certainly not long enough for our exuberance to escape into the prairie sky.

In my middle-of-the-night times I focused on picturing our house without us. It was safer to focus on the quiet house and the barn and all the outbuildings we had explored our first summer there. To picture my brothers and sisters physically hurt my heart.

When we moved into the rented farmhouse, Dad and the landlord had taken us on a tour of the empty structures circling the property so we wouldn't be tempted to examine them on our own. They gave us explicit instructions to stay away from them. Dad drew a line in the gravel driveway—literally picked up a big stick and scraped a line in the dirt. The landlord was there too reinforcing Dad's instructions.

"You oldest ones, you make damn sure your buddies don't go past this line. Is that understood?"

"Yes, sir."

"Especially this pumphouse. And this is why it's dangerous." Dad opened the door of the broken-down shed, its condition belying its importance. Inside was a hole in the floor covered by a rotting wood cover. Under the cover was a deep well filled with water that got pumped into the house. Sometimes Karl or Eric had to run to the pumphouse to "turn the pump on." That phrase reverberated through the house when someone was turning on a faucet and the water pressure dropped. It became a running joke in our family when something malfunctioned. The truck's battery died after church one Sunday, and Jimmy hollered, "Turn the pump on!"

The gravel driveway led from the main road straight towards the barn, past the pumphouse, creating a big circle to accommodate farm equipment. It made a perfect baseball field. Much was off-limits around the perimeter, but it still left us with a gigantic playground and a pasture beside the barn where a horse appeared the previous summer. A distant neighbor boarded the horse named Smoky on our landlord's property. We were all allowed to ride her in exchange for feeding her each morning and night. There was no saddle so one time around the pasture was all I needed. Only Karl and Andy seemed to get the knack of it. I loved to stroke her mane and feed her carrots.

Just as suddenly as she came to us, Smoky disappeared. We came home from school in late October and she didn't trot up to the fence to greet us. Mom said a horse trailer pulled into the circle part of the driveway and she went out to ask what was going on. A guy said they were taking the horse to Colorado. We never got to say goodbye.

The other Grant House:

In my new foster home there was a big picture above the couch of a horse that looked just like Smoky. It made me miss her and feel a kinship with how she got suddenly uprooted. My second foster home was another family named Grant. They were related to the first Grants.

This household was totally different, and only slightly better. I never saw the mother. This Mrs. Grant was ill a lot and rarely came out of her bedroom. Sometimes I wondered if she was really in there. This Mr. Grant was not creepy. He was a sad, quiet man. Connie was in my 8th-grade class and her older sister was in 11th grade. She seemed so much older and was the one who ran the house.

The older sister told me my job was to do the dishes after every meal. Sometimes I wondered who did the dishes before me because they all escaped to the living room to watch TV right after eating. Sunday nights they rushed in to watch the *Ed Sullivan Show*. I used to love watching that show with my dad. I didn't mind missing it now. But one night in February, a new band called *The Beatles* was going to be on. I ran into the living room with the family, but I was not allowed to stay. The older sister whose name I could never remember, was it Marilyn, Marian? She said I had to wash and dry the dinner dishes first. I took my time. Nothing could make me go back in that living room. I could hear the band's loud drumming and strumming as I stood at the kitchen sink, but I never got to see them on TV. Their famous first song always makes me think of dishwater hands.

That first Sunday after the accident I expected to see many of my siblings at church. Five days from the accident and I still only knew where a few of my siblings were.

I counted the minutes until Sunday, awakening early. Sharing a bed with Connie, I tried my best to not move during the night, to make myself small and motionless, hugging the side of the bed. I slowly slid to the floor, careful to keep the covers undisturbed so as not to awaken Connie.

I undressed in the bathroom. The first Mrs. Grant had dropped off the pajamas she had repaired. Of course, I ripped off the button. My clothes were wrinkled because I had worn the same outfit for days in a row. This Mr. Grant promised to drive me to the farmhouse after church so I could retrieve some clothes. Connie said I could pick out an outfit from her closet, but I didn't.

I waited and waited in the Grant's dark living room, focusing on getting to church to see my brothers and sisters. This motherless house was so different from the other Grants. Each hour a clock chimed the time. 7. 8. 9. The house remained quiet. When I couldn't stand it any longer, I walked myself to church. I estimated it to be about three blocks away, with one turn. Two of the blocks were extra long and the wind was extra strong.

As I turned the corner I saw two boys get out of a car and run to opposite sides of the street. The car slowly followed them. I wasn't crying but the cold wind forced my eyes to water and kept me from seeing clearly. I could hear a thud as each rolled up newspaper flew through the air to its doorstop. One boy did the throwing, the other boy on the opposite side of the street, ran up to each house and

81

dropped the paper on the step. He was falling behind. The driver of the car honked his horn.

My vision cleared and I knew the falling-behind-boy was my brother! I recognized his hat that Grandma had knitted. No one else had a hat like it. I ran to the middle of the street to catch up to them, but the boys jumped in the car and it sped off. It had to be Kevin. I was sure the driver had seen me running.

≈

Later Kevin would tell me about his foster home, about Sundays delivering papers, about the grumpy dad, especially grumpy on Sunday mornings when he and the grumpy dad's son had to deliver papers all over town. About how the boys could never do it fast enough, though Kevin had figured out they must be doing it faster with two cutting the work in half. Still, the short-tempered man hollered and scolded.

The first Sunday Kevin approached a house and there at the picture window he saw our sister Katy! He rang the doorbell and saw Karen there too! And then the grumpy guy grabbed Kevin's collar and yelled:

"Don't you ever do that again!" With that he smacked Kevin with a rolled-up newspaper and marched him to the car. Each Sunday Kevin had to deliver the paper to that house. Katy and Karen watched from the picture window, rapping on the glass. Kevin took care not to look directly at them, but raised the newspaper slightly to reveal his waving hand. Then he threw the paper on the porch and ran back to the waiting car.

≈

Now my eyes were freezing from real tears. I ran as fast as I could to the safety of the church. On that first Sunday after the accident, I got there early enough. Only a few older parishioners knelt in their usual pews at the front. The organist was warming up a few choir members. It was the one thing Mom and I got to do together each Sunday, sing in the choir. I couldn't bear to sing today. My plan was to corral each sibling so we could all sit together in our usual pew. I waited and watched in the freezing vestibule, checking each family entering the large front doors, until the choir started singing the first hymn. It didn't make sense. Father Buckley said we all had to be sent to Catholic homes. How come none of my siblings were at church?

I yearned to see Johnny. I needed to explain what happened, that I wasn't allowed to go back to that house and say goodbye to him.

I climbed the back staircase to the choir loft to get a better view of the pews below in case someone had slipped in without my knowing. Only Eric was visible down at the altar. He was the altar boy for this Mass. I retreated down the staircase determined to find my siblings. That's when Mrs. Wengert found me.

She took me in her arms and held me tight. I cried inside my head, but would not show any tears. Mrs. Wengert promised to keep her eye out for each kid, and would go to visit them when she could. She said she would have a talk with Father Buckley.

There were three Masses each Sunday; I decided next Sunday I'd have to attend all three.

The next Sunday I left the Grant's while it was still dark. The earliest Mass started before dawn.

During the week I had been able to fill some of the empty spaces on my list, thanks to Mrs. Wengert:

Karl: the Rileys

Karl stayed with the Riley's, the next farm over. They didn't try to keep tabs on him. He liked to go hunting after school, so he said. But he was really going to feed Pepper and check on the house. At night Karl would wait until the family was asleep and sneak out. He'd traipse across the frozen fields to curl up with Pepper on the couch for a few hours. He'd wake up in time to get back before anyone noticed him missing.

One morning he got back after Mr. Riley had gone to the barn for chores. Karl found a flashlight and a paper bag with extra batteries on the floor where his coat should have been. Mr. Riley never said a word about Karl's middle-of-the-night hikes.

Some weeks later as Karl waited for the household to quiet, he fell asleep and awoke to the whine of Pepper at their back door. Mrs. Riley let her in and let her stay.

It was a good thing because eventually the oil in our furnace ran out and there was no one to pay for a tank refill.

That—our unheated home—would cause repercussions down the road. But for now Karl and Pepper were together.

Patsy: the second Grant family

Eric: the Wengerts

The Wengerts took in Eric. They lived in a spacious house in a new part of town. They were a prominent family in church and in the community. I remember them as very kind and thoughtful and accepting of our family, even before the accident. They were the first to defend us from the gossipers. People making up stories about us seemed to follow us to each new place we moved.

Mrs. Wengert found me at church that first Sunday after the accident. She motioned for me to follow her into the cloakroom. I still couldn't cry, but she could. Wiping tears from her eyes, she told me I could come to their home any time. She knew my situation was not ideal. In less than a week I had been in two homes. She told me she had planned to take both Eric and me, but again Father Buckley intervened. He and Mrs. Wengert had been clashing since he arrived to head the parish two months previously. He had his agenda and he was the boss.

Mrs. Wengert became my touchstone. I looked for her every time I left the Grant's house. If I saw her, I felt like I could make it another day.

She would visit the hospital during the week and tell me hopeful things about Mom. Another church lady would go with her and tell me different stories—how bad Mom looked, how we wouldn't recognize her, she had so many stitches on her face. How it still was touch and go about Mom coming out of the coma.

Mrs. Wengert tried to temper the news about Mom. She gave me hope. And she kept her promise to check on each of my brothers and sisters. She would reassure me that everyone was fine.

I remember asking why none were ever at church but she didn't have an answer.

Andy and Jimmy: the Sebrings

Two-year-old Jimmy cried and cried that first night, finally crying himself to sleep. All was quiet for a few hours, but sometime before dawn Jimmy started crying again. Andy was in the next room and went to his crib to beg him to stop crying. Finally he pulled Jimmy and his blankets out of the crib and together they slept on the floor.

Andy had to go to school and Jimmy started crying again. Mr. Sebring gave Jimmy some chocolate milk and that quieted him for awhile.

Later in the day Mr. Sebring came in from milking cows and Jimmy was crying again. "What's the matter with that kid?" Mr. Sebring hollered. "Somebody give him some chocolate milk, for chrissakes."

Jimmy would cry every day, several times a day. And every day, Mr. Sebring gave him chocolate milk. Before bed Jimmy would get a cup of hot chocolate.

It wasn't like we never had chocolate milk in our house, but it was a special occasion treat. In the Sebring house you could have as much as you wanted, any time you wanted, right inside the milking barn.

Mr. Sebring had found a way to calm Jimmy. He thought Andy might need something too, so he gave him permission to call Karl every week. That first Sunday night all Andy could do was quietly cry into the phone.

There wasn't enough chocolate milk in the barn to stop all the crying.

John: the first Grant family

I knew, but I couldn't bear to think about what John was going through.

Paul: the Ladners

Paul was staying with the Ladners, the family who owned the hardware store. Six-year-old Paul impressed the Ladners with his card-playing ability.

"That kid knows how to play pinochle! He's a six-year-old card shark," Mr. Landner would tell his customers.

Before the accident, during the months when we didn't have a working TV, Dad would organize weekly pinochle tournaments. Paul sat on Dad's lap soaking it all up, until he asked to play on his own. Paul was a cutthroat bidder. In our games someone would often forget to discard the widow, but Paul never did and gleefully passed us by in points. He knew how to seize the momentum and that made him the best partner and a fierce opponent. When we tired of pinochle, and Mom was busy with Sunday dinner, Dad would bring out a different deck of cards, give us a wink, and switch to poker. Paul won the pot of pennies more often than any of us.

Kevin: the Grumpy man
We would find out later what torment he suffered.

Katy and Karen: Doris ??
Katy and Karen were together at a home where the woman's name was Doris. She would stand between the living room and kitchen and point to the doorframe as a way to get my sisters to remember her name: Doris.

Doris had two boys in college but had always wanted a girl. Now she had two, she would tell her neighbors.

Katy and Karen had each other, except when Katy had to go to kindergarten and leave Karen at the picture window quietly crying. That first day the lady dressed Katy for school. Katy tried to tell Doris it wasn't her day for school. The town kids went to kindergarten on Mondays and Wednesdays, farm kids on Tuesdays and Thursdays. Now Katy was a town kid, and all her classmates were strangers.

Phillip: ?? (unknown)
I can't tell you where Phillip was. It torments me even today because I still don't know where he was. My little brother, my buddy, was somewhere, but no one seems to know where.

If I could discover what kind of home he was in, I would be able to complete this story. But his experience is out of reach. He was three years old.

Phillip had never slept a night alone. What must he have felt that first night and all the nights after? Where was his chocolate milk?

Jimmy and Andy: the Sebrings

Beth: the Brennens

Beth was all alone in a houseful of kids and that concerned me. At least I liked the lady taking care of her but one of the boys was in my class and he was a troublemaker. Would Mrs. Brennen know to be alert in the middle of the night for Beth climbing out of her crib? Something bad could happen at 3 a.m.

I sat through three long Masses that second Sunday but I never saw any of my siblings, except Eric.

My final list of foster homes:

Karl	the Rileys
Patsy	the Grants
Eric	the Wengerts
Andy & Jimmy	the Sebrings
John	the other Grants
Paul	the Ladners
Kevin	Grumpy man
Katy & Karen	Doris ??
Phillip	??
Beth	the Brennens

87

CHAPTER 13
Birthday Candles

Winter, 1964
The In-Between Time

That next Sunday I tried to time my walk to church to see the paperboys but I never saw them again. This Sunday, January 19, was especially important. It was Dad's birthday. How could we celebrate? I imagined finding my siblings and together we could kneel at the side altar with the statue of Mary. I wanted us all to remember Dad's birthday and light a candle. Dad didn't like sweets, so a birthday cake was not important to him, but the candle part of the cake was.

Dad especially loved church votive candles, prayer candles he called them. Each Sunday he would take turns giving one of us a quarter. It was our special time to join his ritual of lighting one. He would make a point of explaining how these beeswax candles had a special bell-top design and that let the wax melt evenly and the beeswax burned without smoking. "This quarter will burn for a week. Gives your prayers more time to do their job." Beeswax was too expensive to be used in homes so it became a church ritual, he said, but one requiring a donation.

On this Sunday, Dad's birthday, I waited until the third Mass was over. I had no quarters and I knew it was wrong to light a candle without the donation, but I had started disobeying in small ways—not doing my homework, pretending a headache so I could stay in the nurse's office, skipping class by hiding in the library. On this day, our second Sunday away from home, I lit a dozen candles, one for each of us, in honor of Dad's birthday. When I looked up at the stone statue of the Blessed Mary I felt bad that I had not paid for the candles.

I calculated I owed the church $3.00. Someday I would repay this debt.

I tried to turn away but I seemed to bump up against an invisible curtain and it caused me to turn back to the statue. Mary was made of stone but I swear I felt a wave of warmth envelope me. It went right into me and warmed me from inside. The burning light of 12 dancing flames caught me and held me. Eric had been waiting at the side entrance. He joined me at the altar and whispered, "Father Buckley said you lit too many candles. He said you didn't pay for them."

"I couldn't, Eric. I don't even have a quarter. But it's Dad's birthday. And we always have candles on birthdays."

Eric walked up to the statue and put several coins in the slot. He always had money in his pocket. Dad called him *Moneybags*. He had a knack for finding coins on the ground.

"Mr. Wengert gives me money every week. That should be enough for Father Buckley."

"Thank you, Eric."

"You need any money?"

"I'm okay."

"Here, take this."

I never saw any of my siblings at any of the Masses. Years later I would learn we were not all sent to Catholic homes.

CHAPTER 14
70 Miles

Winter, 1964
The In-Between Time

It was a Saturday morning in February, 25 days after the accident, when there was a knock on the door at the Grant's House. Connie answered.

"It's your brother."

"Come on, Trish, Dad is here. We're going to Glencoe." Karl was the only one who called me *Trish*.

I ran out to a car I didn't recognize.

"Daddy!" This was the first time I had seen him since he was taken back to the hospital. It had been the longest three weeks of my life. Eric was in the back seat and I jumped in the front holding onto Dad as hard as I could.

"Let's get this show on the road! I got the three of you for the weekend."

We would learn Dad had to ask permission to take us out of our foster homes. "Can you believe that? I have to get the okay to see my own kids!"

"How's Mom?" I asked. Not knowing how she was for those 25 days made me think the worst.

"Well, honey, that's where we are going. To the hospital. The doctor thinks it will help her if she can see you. It's not going to be easy because she's not quite the same yet, but that's why we pray."

I was struggling with the idea of prayers right now. Why would a loving God want us to beg for things? And why would some get answered and others not? I was afraid to totally give up on praying, until Mom was out of the woods, but I wasn't finding comfort in church lately. I had been struggling with my confusion at God and anger at Father Buckley. He taught our Religion class one Wednesday night and afterwards I asked him why I didn't see my siblings in church on Sundays. Father scolded me and said I should use my words to pray and not ask questions about things I could not control. I only wanted to know when I could see my brothers and sisters.

Karl was the only one of us old enough to get into the hospital. They had strict rules about children visiting. If you were younger than 14, you could not get past the lobby.

"Just tell them you are 14, Patsy. We'll try to get you in tomorrow, Eric."

Even the doctor told us to fib about our age, said the nurses kind of ran the show. We had to take turns because Mom could only have one visitor a day. She was still coming in and out of her coma. Dad warned me that she slept a lot and didn't always know where she was. He warned us that she might have brain damage. She had a fractured skull and a broken pelvis. They gave her medication to prevent seizures. But Dad didn't warn me about what she would look like—her crushed elbow encased in a huge cast, her leg suspended in traction and worst of all, a face so bandaged and bruised I couldn't tell she was our mom.

The charge nurse took me into the room. I stood alone at the end of Mom's hospital bed. She didn't move. I was afraid to touch her, she looked so fragile. A few minutes later the nurse came to lead me out of the room. Mom had not moved.

"It's better that she didn't wake up. She doesn't want to see you."

I was crushed, and too stunned to say anything. When I made my way back to the lobby I cried out to Dad: "Why doesn't Mom want to see me?"

"Why would you say that?"

"The nurse did. Mommy didn't wake up, but the nurse said the doctor was wrong to have me come."

"Dammit, there's always one," Dad said.

"She also said I didn't belong here. I wasn't old enough for this."

"Wait here with your brothers. I'll be right back."

I don't know what Dad said or did, but after that all of us got to visit Mom's room together and we didn't have to deal with that nurse again, though she glared each time she saw us. That night we shared Dad's motel room. He had sleeping bags for us and that motel room floor was the coziest bed I'd had in weeks.

The next day was Sunday and Dad got us up early for Mass, then we got to go out for breakfast at a local truck stop. Everyone seemed to know who Dad was and when the bill came, someone at the counter reached over to pay it.

At the hospital we stood around Mom's bed but she still did not wake up. It was hard to see her like that. After a few minutes Dad took us to Grandma and Grandpa's room down the hall. Grandma was sitting up eating her breakfast and Grandpa was sleeping in the bed by the window, his fake wooden leg propped in a corner.

"How's my daughter doing?" Grandma asked Dad.

"About the same."

Grandma looked so good to me. I was relieved she didn't have any visible bandages. She asked me to sit beside her on the bed. "Don't worry, I won't break. These ribs are healing up nicely." Dad didn't want us to wake up Grandpa, so he sent the boys to the lobby. I sat stiffly next to Grandma. With all my might I wanted to fold myself into her arms but I knew it would make me cry and I knew I wouldn't be able to stop.

Grandma had been a nurse for many years so the hospital let her stay as a patient to help with Grandpa. They both got discharged soon after.

"You be brave, little one, your Dad needs you to be brave," Grandma waved goodbye. I knew where the lobby was by now. When I got there I was surprised to see Mr. and Mrs. Wengert. They had been coming every Sunday since the accident to check on Mom. Mrs. Wengert took me aside.

"I know it's hard to see your mom like that, but she is improving each time I come."

"The nurse said Mom doesn't want to see me."

"Of course your mom wants to see you. But maybe the nurse thinks the scars will scare you."

I felt comforted by Mrs. Wengert's words but when the night terrors would awaken me, it was the nurse's words I had taken to bed with me.

"Your mom doesn't want to see you."

Every Friday night for the next two months Dad would pick us up. Karl, Eric and I got to spend the weekend with him. Mom was more wakeful the next time we visited. Doctors were encouraged by her progress. Luckily, she didn't seem to have any obvious brain damage; her eye drooped and she suffered with double vision, but she talked like our mom. She didn't laugh for the longest time and that was hard to take.

Every Sunday afternoon Dad drove us the 70 miles back to Granite Falls. I knew we were close to town when the highway took a deep dive down a steep hill. On the edge of town where the river joined the highway a dark cloud of sadness seemed to enter the car and I breathed it in. I dreaded each mile that brought me closer to the Grant's front door.

After Dad dropped us off that Sunday, he made the rounds to the homes of the rest of the kids. The next week Father Buckley told Dad the kids cried too much when he left; some of the foster parents asked that he not come back. The Sebrings organized a picnic at their farm in February so my brothers and sisters could see each other, but Dad wasn't invited. "Can you believe that? I can't even go and see my own kids?" Dad honored the request, by choice or decree I'm not sure, but I could sense his growing dislike of Father Buckley. Dad always respected each priest he encountered, but he was beginning to distrust this one.

Soon after, Father Buckley put the kibosh on future picnics. He said it was too disruptive for the youngest ones to settle back in to a routine at their foster homes.

Hold dear to your parents for it is a scary and confusing world without them.
— **Emily Dickinson**

It's been said:
To understand your trauma you must
return to the first traumatic memory you have.
Thus our journey back to 1955.

CHAPTER 15
Mom Said . . .

1955 Kansas City

"You're gonna get polio if you don't take a nap. How many times do I have to say it?"

"But I'm not tired, Mom. Not even a little." I argued with her every day and every day she would say: "You need your rest. It's doctor's orders."

"Charlie Conway says that's a lie, Mom. You can't get polio from *not* taking a nap."

Charlie Conway was our next-door neighbor, sandwiched between Larry Demmel and us. They were our playmates and every summer day they would meet us in our backyard after we emerged from naptime and we'd play together until nightfall. Larry and Charlie and Karl and Eric and me. Eric was the youngest of us all, a year behind me, and I was a year behind Karl, who was a summer away from starting first grade. Larry and Charlie had just finished second grade, but they didn't seem that old. Karl somehow had become the leader of us all, of everything. Larry and Charlie didn't like it that they had to wait till our naptime was over to get our baseball game going.

"So, Charlie is calling your mother a liar, is he?" Mom asked in a rising voice.

"Larry said so, too, Mom. Larry's mom said that was ridiculous what you told us about polio," said Karl. "Larry's mom never makes him take a nap and he hasn't gotten polio."

"Well, I know somebody who did," said Eric who didn't mind sleeping in the daytime.

"Prove it," said Karl.

97

"I heard Aunt Helen say it. So there." Eric had heard our cousin's classmate had to live in an iron lung.

We saw one on TV once. An Iron Lung. It was a great big steel machine that took up a whole room. Mom got pictures from a magazine at the library that held us captive with images of gigantic tombs of steel where tiny heads emerged from one end. She read to us from the article about how the children had to live the rest of their lives in a sanitarium, left there by their families, trapped inside a metal monster. It was enough to make you want to sleep for a month of Sundays. No more playing baseball for these kids. That would be our fate if we didn't take a nap every afternoon in hot July. Mom said.

"That's not the first time Larry Demmel has said something he shouldn't," said Mom. "You tell Larry for me, until he has five kids of his own, he can keep his opinions to himself. Dr. Langis said you all need a nap or you'll get polio. That's good enough for me."

That's not what I remembered Dr. Langis saying. "Della," he said to Mom as he stood over me. He motioned for his nurse with the long, very long and very thick needle, to stab my arm with the polio vaccine. "Della, make sure the kids eat well and sleep well. That's about all we can do. We don't even know if these shots work yet."

That fateful conversation became Mom's edict: We all had to lie down after lunch every day and take a nap. I think Mom just wanted to take a nap herself. All five of us kids plus Mom would gather in our parents' big bed. Mom and the babies would go first, their rhythmic, easy breathing taking them to a place that eluded me. Only the vision of the young child immobilized in a monster metal chamber kept me still. In the end I always, finally, fell asleep.

None of us ever got polio, but Mom couldn't protect us from everything.

CHAPTER 16
Five by Five

1955 Kansas City

Everything about the day was upside down. It was a Thursday and Dad should have been on the road, but he and his boss Harv had flown back from New York a day early. We wouldn't be making our weekly trip to the airport to pick him up.

The phone rang while we were at the breakfast table on that Thursday morning. We could hear Dad's voice booming on the other end. "The head honcho called us back home, Hon. We took an early flight and a cab to the office. Something important's shaking. I'll be home later tonight."

Johnny squirmed in his highchair. Andy was perched on the hefty Kansas City phone book so he could reach the table. He dropped Cheerios on the floor for Pepper.

We were a family of five kids in 1955. Karl was five; I was four, Eric three, Andy two, and Johnny one. Mom was pregnant with Baby #6. Paul would be born exactly three months later.

Mom finished talking to Dad as we waited to be excused from the table. The swingset and sandbox were calling to us.

"Okay, kids," Mom clapped to get our attention. "First, will you all help me freshen up the house? Your father's coming home today."

"Daddy's coming home! Daddy's coming home!"

"But it's only Thursday," Eric said.

"Well, I guess that makes it an upside-down kind of day, wouldn't you say?" Mom seemed to perk up. It had been an especially long, hot week. She was still suffering from an extended bout of morning sickness. I had caught her whispering into the phone that morning, wiping her eyes.

"Mom, what's wrong?" I asked and she quickly hung up the phone.

"Nothing, dear," Mom turned to me with one of her put-on smiles. "It's just this baby is kicking so much, he's giving me a stomachache."

"Why do you say *he*?" I asked. "We have enough boys. I want a sister!"

"It could be a girl. We'll know in September." But it wasn't to be. My fifth brother was giving Mom a hard time.

Her queasy stomach explained why she hadn't eaten breakfast with us. Karl had already darted through the kitchen door and was halfway across the long screened-in porch before Mom called him back.

"Where do you think you're going, mister? I just asked you to help clean up."

"But, Mom, you *asked* us if we could help. You didn't say we *had* to. Why can't my answer be I wanna go outside?"

"Oh, honey," Mom sighed and looked around to address all of us. "That was not a request, that is what is called a *polite demand.* Understood?"

"But, Mom, I have to go find the ball we lost in the back 40 last night before the neighbor kids take it."

"No *buts* about it, Karl Edward. You get your butt back in here, young man, and help us freshen up." We knew what *freshen-up* meant—a full-on deep clean.

I learned something new that morning, thanks to Karl. Mom was always asking, for example: "Would you mind folding these towels?" I was always tempted to answer: "Yes, I would mind." Now, I knew better. Later, when I asked Dad about *polite demands* he said it was Mom's Minnesota way—asking sideways.

For now we had to make our beds and throw all the dirty laundry down the basement staircase. Mom put the babies, Andy and Johnny, in the bathtub with a wet sponge so they could be busy while she scrubbed the floor.

Mom seemed happier than she had been all week. She even sat down with us at lunchtime. We had almost finished our peanut butter and jelly sandwiches when Pepper perked up her ears and ran to the door, scratching at the screen. Karl let her out.

"It's a big truck, Mom!" A delivery man stood at the front gate, afraid to open it.

"Pepper, go lay down," Mom commanded and Pepper immediately obeyed.

The man handed a large package in bright-colored paper to Karl and Eric. "It's breakable," he said. "Don't drop it." They carefully carried the package to the kitchen. Mom told us all to keep our hands away from the table while she unwrapped the paper, revealing a crystal vase filled with tall red roses.

An envelope fluttered to the floor. Eric picked it up and opened it. Inside was a letter and a check. "Look. Mom! It's a $100!" Eric couldn't read but he knew his numbers and dollar signs.

"I haven't had roses delivered since your father forgot my birthday the year we were married."

We loved to hear Mom tell that story and we'd clamor to hear Dad's version. But that would have to wait. Mom read the letter to herself and put it back in the envelope with Dad's handwriting on the front. She dabbed at her eyes with her apron.

"What's wrong, Mom?"

"Oh, these are happy tears, honey. Your father got a big promotion at work. We are having steak tonight!"

"Was that why you got that check?" asked Eric.

Karl figured we should make a list of things we could buy with it. "How 'bout we get a swimming pool?"

"Okay, kids, it's naptime. We'll make it a short one today. You've earned it."

CHAPTER 17
Andy's Hand

June 30, 1955
Kansas City

After naptime, and long before dinner we were out playing in Larry's yard, right past Charlie's house. We were not supposed to be in Larry's yard. It wasn't an actual rule, it's just that Charlie and Larry and any other kids on our street always came to the Kahmann house to play. We had the biggest yard, the best sandbox, the sturdiest swingset and the only manicured baseball field, created every spring by Dad and his lawnmower.

But this was still the upside-down day and for some reason the ice cream man stopped his van in front of Larry's house instead of ours and we took off running to make sure we didn't miss him before he jingled his way down the street. Karl got there first because he could run faster than anyone. The ice cream man always gave the first kid and the last kid the biggest scoop. Eric, being the youngest of our group, got in line last, but Larry shoved him forward so Larry could get the big scoop. The ice cream man was busy making change and could not have seen what happened, but he gave Larry a scrawny cone anyway and handed Eric his favorite, a fudgsicle. That was my favorite too.

And then we just wandered to the back of Larry's house where we ate our treats in his sandbox. This was the first time we had ever gathered in Larry's yard. We always played in our own backyard. That way we could keep an eye on the babies, Andy and Johnny. I only remember playing in Larry's sandbox that one time, the 30th day of June, 1955.

Eric bit into his hard fudgsicle like it was nothing. I had to turn away; it hurt my teeth just to watch him do that. If I didn't wait for mine to soften up, the frosty cold would send a pain right up behind my eyes, causing tears to spill out and I'd have to pretend to be picking sand out of my chocolate, so the boys wouldn't think I was crying.

"Where's Andy?" asked Eric, looking around.

"I don't know. I thought you had him," said Karl.

"I don't have him."

"He was on your porch when we left," Charlie said.

Andy had his second birthday in late April and though he wanted to be one of us big kids, he could never keep up. I'd see him sneak off to the porch steps and suck his thumb. He had his own way about it. He would put his little hand all the way in his mouth and then pull it out until just his thumb was left. And then he would look around quickly to see if anyone was watching. Sometimes he would fall asleep on the back porch steps that way.

"He was with your dad, Charlie." Karl said. Andy liked to follow Mr. Conway around when he was tinkering in his garage. That kept him out of our hair.

"Mom'll be mad if we left him behind," said Eric.

"He didn't want to come," said Charlie. "Besides, why do you always have to watch the babies?"

"Andy's not a baby. He's two years old, for chrissake," said Karl. "Johnny's the baby."

"Yeah, Johnny's the baby cuz he sucks his thumb."

"Shut up, Larry."

"Andy sucks his thumb, too, so that makes him a baby," said Charlie.

"He does not," Karl defended.

"He does, too."

"Does not."

"I seen him," said Charlie. "He sticks his whole hand in his mouth until he 'bout chokes himself."

"What do you know about babies?" said Karl, raising his voice.

"You never had any babies in your house. Except you. You're an Only Child!" Karl knew that was an insult.

"Well, your mom has 'em all the time. How come your mom has so many babies, huh?"

"I saw Andy climbing the sandpile next to the cement mixer," Larry said. "He's not supposed to be there. Our mom won't let us play on that sandpile. It's for the cement your dad's mixing." Mr. Conway had borrowed our dad's cement mixer. The pile of sand was left over from Dad's latest project and we were given strict instructions not to go near it.

The scream came in the midst of this and sliced through the air like a hatchet. I can remember my fudgsicle flying out of my hand, as if someone had yanked it away. With four brothers, a big dog, and daily games of Cowboys-and-Indians, we were used to death-defying shrieks. But this was a sound like none other.

Eric jumped up, dropping his ice cream in the sand. "That sounds like Andy."

"No, it was Johnny."

"It was not. I tell you that was Andy."

When Eric knew something, he knew it and no one dared argue. He had an authority in his voice, even as an almost four-year-old, that you didn't mess with. He didn't use it very often—that authority—but when he did, he was always right.

"Let's go," Eric commanded.

And we took off. Karl, Larry, and Charlie ran across the back yards to our house. Eric circled around towards the front and I followed him. It wasn't that far and we were fast runners, but still things were happening ahead of us. It felt like we were moving through water. We couldn't run fast enough.

Mrs. Mathis was standing in the middle of the street. I could see Mom running towards Mr. Conway's car, which had somehow appeared in our driveway. Mom in her new maternity top with her apron still on. Dad was behind her holding one of the babies to his chest. Dad's shirtsleeve hid the baby's face. We still didn't know if it was Johnny or Andy. Dad's starched white shirt was red up by his shoulder.

Mr. Conway squealed his car out of the driveway and down the street, taking Mom and Dad and one of the babies with him.

I could hear Johnny screaming in his playpen. It was a different kind of scream than we had just heard. It was a baby-kind of scream. Not a nightmare-forming scream. That meant it had to be Andy in Daddy's arms.

Eric and I stood in the driveway and stared at blood stains on the new concrete. The front door to our house sprang open with Larry, Charlie, and Karl spilling out, peering intently at the splotches of blood.

"Your brother got his hand cut off," screamed Charlie. "In the cement mixer."

"At the wrist." Larry added, bent over trying to catch his breath.

Mrs. Mathis ordered us into the house and said we were forbidden to go outside because of the cement mixer. Still, we followed the trail of blood all the way across our long back porch. We could see Andy's shoe on the steps. Karl eased the screen door open and grabbed the shoe. It was stained red. "I bet there's lots of blood back there." Larry pointed to the sandpile. Had to be. There must be so much blood out by the cement mixer that cut off Andy's hand. At the wrist.

Charlie whispered, "My mom said his hand was only held on by a piece of skin."

"Shut up, Charlie," I said. Why did Charlie have to say that? It's worse than picturing it cut cleanly. His baby hand hanging by a piece of skin. And blood. How will I ever be able to *not* see that? For the longest time whenever I'd close my eyes, all I could see was a hand, flopping senselessly, gushing blood all over the ground.

And then there was Daddy's crisp, white shirt. As Eric and I ran to the front of the house I saw Dad with a baby sprinting from our front door to Mr. Conway's car. Even from a distance I could see it, the bright red marks on his collar, on the shoulder, down the front of his shirt. I didn't want to believe that's what I had seen. I didn't want it to be Andy. I didn't want it to be Johnny, either. Make it be someone else's brother. Please.

Later that night I thought I should be crying. But I couldn't make it happen. Even when I found the envelope.

CHAPTER 18
The Envelope

June 30, 1955
Kansas City

I found the envelope later that night underneath the kitchen table. It wasn't addressed to me, but I opened it anyway. I didn't know it was wrong to read other people's mail. It probably didn't matter anyway. Things had turned upside down all day and into the night. It was the letter from Dad to Mom that arrived with the vase of roses. This was the letter that gave Mom happy tears.

My Dearest Darling,
   Enclosed is a token for your own personal use. The going gets pretty rough at times but it's moments like this that bring a little sunshine into the path of our troubles and worries.
   All of my gains are your gains just as all of my failures are shared by you also. May we thank God that it will always be this way together—everything shared as one.
   Thank you, My Darling, for boosting me along the way.
   Yours always and in all ways
   All My Love,
   Jack

   P.S. ONE CONDITION — Money cannot be spent on anything but yourself.

Mom had a sewing machine console and I took her letter with me as I found my hiding place underneath the part of the sewing machine where your feet go.

When Mom wasn't using it, she would push a lever and the sewing arm folded in on itself, disappearing into the console, transforming magically into a desk. The space underneath was just big enough for a five-year-old to hide, as long as you didn't accidently press on the foot pedal that would make a telltale sound. It was cramped underneath but I felt it was my job to wait for Andy, to stand guard by the front door. I folded my hands in prayer the way Daddy would do and wished with my whole body that God would hear my silent pleading: Fix Andy's hand. Please, please, please! So help me, I promise, we will never leave Andy behind again. Who cares if he sucks his thumb? We will let him be with us older kids any time he wants.

Mrs. Mathis didn't know of my hiding place. She sat on the couch just a few feet away. I thought she looked right at me but she didn't seem to see me. There had been a lot of commotion all night, neighbors coming in and out of our front door.

Karl became our spokesman and kept asking Mrs. Mathis when they would be home. After a while she didn't seem to hear him. I saw all this from my vantage point inside the sewing machine desk. I saw Karl pick up the black telephone and put his finger in one of the circles on the dial. He had a year of school behind him and knew how to dial Aunt Helen's number. You could hear the busy signal across the room.

I don't remember eating supper but I had emerged from my hiding place to watch Mrs. Mathis wash and dry the dishes. It was past our bedtime but she didn't make us go to bed. At one point Karl ushered us all into Mom and Dad's room. With Andy missing there was a big hole in the middle of us, where he belonged. From the time he could lift his head as an infant, Andy spent his waking hours making us laugh. Dad said every family has one: the clown, the joker, the one with moxie. That was Andy. Karl sat on the edge of the bed. Eric tucked Johnny under the covers and sang to him. That's when I made my move and headed back to my secret hiding place.

"Where do you think you're going?" Karl tried to block my way. "We should stay together."

"I'm going to wait for them by the front door."

"Patsy, they won't be home tonight."

"Why, Karl?" But he didn't answer me. I slid into my hiding place so I could be the first to jump out and scream, "Boo!" to welcome Andy home. I knew that would make him laugh and that would make us all laugh after this long upside-down day.

There was lots of thinking time in my hiding place. Andy was no longer a baby technically because Johnny had come along but still had a bottle at bedtime. I couldn't wait to put my arms around him and tell him he could sleep in my bed so he wouldn't wake up scared. Andy was too young to know, like I knew, that sometimes the nurses take you away from your mom and make you lie on a cold tall table and stick needles in you.

I wished I had brought a pillow with me. My eyes were on fire but when I tried to close them, the dangling hand appeared.

I heard a car door slam and a voice and then our front door swung open, blocking my view. Finally they're home! But no, it was Mrs. Conway who had barged in without knocking. She closed the door and looked around the room but didn't see me.

"Oh, Doris," she said to Mrs. Mathis. "It's awful." Mrs. Conway had just returned by cab from the hospital. "Richard drove so fast. I can't tell you how many red lights he ran. But no cops caught up to us. The surgeon had to come from another hospital. Finally around 8:00 the surgery began. They said it's going to be a long night so Richard hailed a taxi for me and said he would stay." Mrs. Conway paced in front of my hiding place. "They put Della in a hospital room. Seemed afraid she'd go into labor. You know, she's had a tough time with this one."

"That poor woman," said Doris. "How does she do it?"

"Well, they're Catholic, you know." I was hearing too much in my hiding place. "Richard feels terrible. He said he knows for sure he turned it off when he was finished. The cement mixer. He remembers shouting at Andy to go play with the other kids."

"Accidents happen, Lois. Nobody's fault. So many kids to keep track of," Mrs. Mathis said. "How did it happen?"

"Richard said the switch is down low. It looks like a light switch. Andy must have watched him flip the switch. You know how kids are. Richard says it must have been the fan belt that sliced through his wrist. The doctor is trying to save his hand, but first they have to save his life. "

"He must have lost a lot of blood."

"Oh, Doris, Richard was in the cafeteria with Jack when a priest came in. Jack's bloody shirt was quite the sight and everyone in the hospital knew something big was going on. The priest said: 'You must be the father of the boy who lost his hand.' Jack screamed at him: 'He has not lost his hand! Dr. McCoy is working on him right now.' But the priest insisted: 'Well, I was in the operating room, the observation deck. I tell you something, I saw his hand on a gurney and his body on the operating table next to it. Saw it. It was completely off.'"

The ringing phone saved me from hearing any more horrible things. I slipped out of my hiding place and ran to Karl. "I think I'm going to throw up!"

"No, you're not. Don't be a baby."

Pepper whimpered from her perch next to Johnny and Eric, who had fallen asleep. "Karl, she needs to go out."

"We'd better take her to the front. Keep her away from the blood in the backyard."

I remember Karl and I taking Pepper outside in the dark. I remember seeing the neighbor ladies sitting at the kitchen table and I remember telling all I heard. "What's a fan belt, Karl?"

I remember climbing up on Mom and Dad's bed, and coaxing Pepper to lay beside me so I could stroke her silky fur. Because of Pepper I could finally close my eyes without seeing the hand. At some point in the night Pepper whimpered and woke me up. Miss Millie Bea was standing over me.

"Where's Andy? Where's Mommy?"

"There, there, PatsyGail. Your momma's at the hospital with your brother."

"Where's my Daddy?"

"Your Daddy was here to change his clothes. He just left to go back to be with them. I'm here now and I plan to make y'all some pancakes. As soon as the sun comes up."

110

Miss Millie had never come before breakfast. She sometimes stayed overnight and we'd wake to the sound of bacon in the frying pan. Mom made bacon in the broiler.

But Miss Millie never came in the middle of the night. She gathered me up on her lap, rocking me back and forth. "There, there. Everything's gonna be all right."

I loved the feel of Miss Millie Bea's arms around me, but I wanted it to be Mom holding me, telling me Andy was okay. I looked around the big bed. Karl, Eric, and Johnny were still asleep. Pepper had left my side and was on the floor by the patio door. She lifted her head and I ran to her, nuzzling my cheek in her fur.

That's when I saw it. Pepper had been lying on top of Daddy's bloody shirt.

Check:

No. 2427
Mr. or Mrs. John E. Kahmann
R. R. No. 12
Kansas City 16, Missouri

Kansas City, Mo. June 30, 1955   18-127/1010

Pay to the Order of Mrs. Della M. Hohman $100.00

One Hundred and no/100 — Dollars

Grand Avenue Bank
of Kansas City, Missouri

John E. Hohman

My Dearest Darling,

Enclosed is a token for your own personal use. The going gets pretty rough at times but it's moments like this that bring a little sunshine into the path of our trouble and worries.

All of my gains are your gains first or all of my failures are shared by you also; may we thank God that it will always be this way together — everything shared as one.

Thank you my Daling for boosting me along the way.

Yours always in all ways
all my love
Jock

P.S. ONE CONDITION — money cannot be spent on anything but yourself.

Jock.

CHAPTER 19
Almost Famous

1955-1962 Kansas City

Through bits and pieces of overheard phone conversations and whispering adults, and later from Mom herself, we pieced together what happened before and after the scream.

Mom was cooking dinner and Dad had come in the front door. "I went to meet him with a kiss and a big thank-you hug for the flowers. And then we heard it." From the kitchen they saw Andy lying on the ground. Dad sprinted across the long back porch, jumping from the top steps to the ground, running to Andy.

"Della! I need a dishtowel!"

"When he came in the back door he got the towel from me and put a tourniquet on Andy's upper arm and held his hand in place. We ran out the front door. Richard and Lois put us in their car."

Dad held Andy over his shoulder in the passenger seat so he could see Mom. She was able to stroke his face and keep him calm. "Andy never cried. Never made a peep."

Mr. Conway drove "like a bat out of hell" to get to the closest doctor's office in Gladstone. Dad ran in with Andy. "It's off!" he screamed at the doctor.

Mom had run in with Dad and watched the doctor release the tourniquet Dad had fashioned with a dishtowel. "We have to keep the blood flowing. I can't save this hand, but Dr. McCoy might be able to," the doctor said, re-tightening the tourniquet and wrapping Andy's hand together with Dad's as a type of splint. "I took classes from him. It's a good thing you came here first. The closest hospital would have quickly amputated it."

Mom felt momentarily relieved, too stunned to question why they had driven to a doctor's office. "I didn't think Richard Conway knew how bad Andy's hand was."

The Gladstone doctor ordered his nurse to call for a police escort. "There's no time for an ambulance. Go! They'll catch up to you!"

The only hospital equipped to handle this type of trauma was St. Joseph's in downtown Kansas City, a half-hour drive. The only doctor who could tackle this was performing an emergency surgery across town at another hospital.

Dr. Frederick McCoy was a gifted plastic surgeon who had many prominent clients from across the country. During his army days he had reconstructed damaged faces and mangled bodies. No one had ever successfully reattached a severed limb but he had reattached an ear and he held out the belief that it was merely a matter of time before it would be done.

That Thursday Dr. McCoy had just finished a full day of surgeries, the final one a complicated procedure on a woman who had battery acid thrown in her face. Then he was summoned to another dire surgery in another hospital 20 miles away.

"The drive to the hospital sticks in my mind," Mom said. "All the traffic lights were green. Except one. It turned from yellow to red and the car in front stopped. Richard drove up on the sidewalk, swerving around cars and the traffic light pole, to get through the intersection. We crossed the ASB Bridge and a cop in the opposite direction made a U-turn. He caught up with us at the hospital."

The ER staff had been alerted and swarmed the car, trying to take Andy from Dad but he screamed so fiercely Mom insisted they stop. It was the only time Andy cried. Mom waved off the waiting gurney and cupped her hand over Andy's eyes to calm him from the sea of white coats and helped Dad carry him through the open doors.

Once inside they were barraged with questions. One doctor looked at Andy and asked, "How did this happen, kid?"

Mom stopped him. "This is a baby! You cannot question him. Get out of here."

A kindly resident looked gingerly at Mom and said she could hold Andy while he inserted an IV. Dad and Andy were still splinted together.

When Dr. McCoy finally made it to the hospital, he took a moment to hold Mom's hand and looked directly at Dad. "I will do everything in my power to save your son's hand. But you have to make a promise to me. You will not—for one instant—feel guilty for what happened today. Kids can disappear when we blink. I see it all the time. The best gift you can give your kids is to take that burden off your shoulders."

Dr. McCoy sedated Andy while Mom was holding him. Only when Andy was completely unconscious did the doctor untether him from Dad and gently pry him from Mom's arms. That's when he noticed Mom was very pregnant. "Nurse, get this woman a hospital bed! This little boy is going to need her." Dr. McCoy himself carried Andy into the operating room.

Dad paced outside the surgery doors hour after hour, no longer believing they were trying to save Andy's hand. Despite the doctor's promise, Dad had been told it wasn't to be. A priest stopped Dad in the cafeteria, noticing his bloody shirt, and told him he witnessed the operation and they were sewing up the stump. "Let us pray they can still save his life."

Dad turned to Richard, "I'm going in there!"

Richard and an intern held Dad back, "Don't listen to the priest," the intern shouted. "He doesn't even have scrubs on."

But Dad couldn't be sure. "Why would a priest lie?"

Richard paced with Dad and kept his thoughts to himself. He felt that something wasn't making sense, that stitching up an amputation should not be taking this long. The night dragged on and Dad was mostly quiet except for mentioning an army buddy who had his mangled leg amputated. "It didn't take this long, Richard." Six hours and many pints of blood later, Dr. McCoy emerged from the operating room, with his mask hanging at his neck.

"My team just witnessed a miracle," Dr. McCoy quietly said.

"Is my son ALIVE?!"

"Oh, yes, that little tyke is going to live a long life. With two strong hands."

"How can that be?" cried Dad.

"Doctor," Richard said. "A priest told us Andy's hand was totally off, laying on another table. He prayed with Jack here and said he saw you stitching up the end of his arm."

"Oh, God, him again." Dr. McCoy held onto Dad's shoulders. "Look at me. There was no priest in the operating room. Your son was never separated from his hand. There was a narrow flap of skin still attached. And that's what guided me to put it all back together. I believe we did it."

Dr. McCoy took Dad and Richard to a secluded office and pulled out a bottle of whiskey. "I think you could use this." He explained the next few hours would be critical, but as long as Andy's fingers stayed pink, that meant the tiny veins were holding strong and able to circulate fresh blood through his hand.

Andy missed our Fourth of July celebration. We all piled in the station wagon that night and Dad drove us to the hospital so we could light sparklers in the parking lot and hope they could be seen on the seventh floor.

Dr. McCoy thought it was important to release Andy as soon as possible, but the medical team thought he should stay where he could be protected. "Jack, I'm fighting with the powers-that-be. I think Andy needs to be at home. Healing is more than physical."

Dr. McCoy won and Andy would be coming home within a week. But before Mom would hear the news, she overheard nurses talking in the elevator.

"Did you hear about that little boy that got his hand cut off?"

"Of course, it's all over the hospital."

"Isn't it a shame though. That boy will grow up with a baby hand?"

Mom couldn't believe what she was hearing. Dr. McCoy was due to come to Andy's room for his rounds, but Mom marched down the hall looking for him. "What have you done to my son?" Mom cried when she found the doctor coming from a patient's room.

"What are you talking about? He's going home tomorrow!"

Dr. McCoy steered Mom into an empty room as she explained what she had overheard about Andy's hand never growing. "They said he's going to be a grown man with a baby hand!"

"What in the world? I had to tell your husband the same thing. Never listen to hospital gossip. The grapevine is in overdrive. It's because your son is a miracle. I've always been straight with you. As long as there is no infection, his hand will grow with the rest of him."

Andy's bandage was bigger than his body, layers of gauze covering his entire arm. It was too early to put a cast on it. They had to be alert for any signs of infection, ready to go back in for more surgery if necessary.

Andy's homecoming was exciting and scary. We had strict instructions to protect Andy's hand at all costs. Even Pepper knew and hovered day and night. We brought every pillow we owned to the couch to surround Andy.

Dad joked that on his next trip to New York he'd have to bring a bigger suitcase. "To hell with hotel towels," Dad laughed. "I better stuff my suitcase with those thick pillows."

Luckily Miss Millie Bea had come into our lives that summer because without her it would have been impossible to keep Andy occupied and stationary.

Karl, Eric, and I took turns sleeping on the floor beside the couch just in case Andy tried to get up in the night or accidently roll off. Karl would teach Andy to recite poetry; I would read Andy's favorite picture book, *Lucky Mrs. Ticklefeather*; Eric would turn up the radio when a popular song came on and they would sing it together over and over until Mom called out: "Change the station!" Andy was a quick learner. When he went to his doctor visits—and there were many that summer—he'd toddle down the hospital corridor waving his bandaged hand like a conductor:

"*16 tons and whadda get. Another day older and deeper in debt. St. Peter dontcha call me cuz I can't goooo. I owe my soul to the company store.*"

During the day Miss Millie shooed Mom out of the kitchen and made her sit with her feet propped up, next to Andy. "Miss Della, you sit quiet now. You're in the family way and we gotta keep an eye on you too. Mister Andy, you holler if your momma tries to get outta that chair."

We kept Johnny outside with us, but he didn't like it much. He was only a year old and couldn't keep up, so we carried him all around the yard. We had learned our lesson—he would never be out of our sight.

The morning after Andy's accident there was so much commotion in our house. We heard the neighbors would be in our backyard carting the cement mixer and sandpile away. Before that happened we had to see it. Karl gave us a signal. Eric and I snuck out the front door and raced around to the back where it loomed over us in the corner of the yard, the cement mixer. Eric crouched down following the trail of blood from the fanbelt to the sandpile and all the way up the back steps. Soon a rainstorm would wash it all away but that corner of the yard would always hold a cold fascination to it.

After a few weeks Andy had an important doctor appointment. He would be getting the stitches out and Dr. McCoy would finally see the outcome of that late-night, six-hour surgery. As each layer of gauze came away Mom almost fainted, but it was Dad they had to find a chair for. If you didn't look at the angry stitches on his wrist, Andy's hand was pink and almost like his left hand.

Dr. McCoy had tears in his eyes, Mom would tell us later, with tears in her own. Dr. McCoy said the *Kansas City Star* wanted to do a story on this miracle baby and take pictures of Andy and the family.

Dad sat us all down that night and told us there would be no story in the paper. Dr. McCoy's groundbreaking surgery would be chronicled in the medical literature as the first successful limb reattachment, but Dad would not give his permission to the reporters.

"No kid of mine is going to be treated like a freak. That's what reporters do."

"But, Dad, we could show the headline to our friends at school. Our brother is famous."

"You can tell your friends, but there will be no reporters."

Once a year Dad would let Andy accompany Dr. McCoy to a medical lecture at the University where he would show the students and visiting surgeons Andy's hand, fully functioning, growing normally. There was a wide scar that wrapped around his wrist, except for the top where the flap of skin had stayed connected.

Years later there would be a dispute about the claim of being the first. But for that flap of skin, Dr. McCoy couldn't officially claim Andy as the first complete limb reattachment. Dad would later have mixed feelings about not letting the reporters tell the full story.

For the longest time Andy insisted on wearing long sleeves, even in the summer. Later, when we'd stand in stairstep formation for a family picture, Andy would hide his "bum hand," as we called it, behind whoever stood next to him. Over time the scar eased its rage and began to soften. You really couldn't tell his hand was anything but normal unless Andy let you look closely, which he never did.

Mom took the $100 check that Dad had given her and tucked it away. "We were worried about all the medical costs that summer, so I didn't cash it. We thought the expense of such a top surgeon would be enormous." Dr. McCoy never sent a bill.

Mom hated roses after that. It was obvious why, but others thought it couldn't be true. "You must be joking. How can anyone hate roses?" people would ask if the subject came up and, oddly, it often came up.

"I am *not* kidding," Mom would say. "Roses are lovely, of course, but when I see that delivery truck pull into the driveway, I know a calamity is coming." Even before first grade I knew what calamity meant.

I started first grade that fall and got in trouble the first week. Karl had warned me I wouldn't like school so much. "Just pray you don't get Sister Rose Dorothy. She's mean. Mad-dog mean. And I'm here to tell ya, there's no fixin' mean." Karl had turned seven in August, but talked like an old man. He liked to pretend he was a hillbilly from the Ozarks.

If I got Sister Rose Dorothy I would show Karl. I would be her best student. The first week of school my teacher sashayed swiftly to my desk and grabbed the yellow crayon out of my hand. Sister Rose Dorothy had pointed to a vase of fake flowers and told us to draw the roses.

119

"But my mother hates roses," I blurted out, forgetting the rule of raising our hand before speaking.

"Your mother does not hate roses. Why would you say such a thing? Now get out your red crayon."

I didn't even know how to draw roses. I was only five when I started first grade. We didn't have kindergarten where we lived. I was the youngest in our class and everyone was taller, but I didn't care. I knew I was meant to be in this magical place called *school*, but Sister Rose Dorothy had to go and ruin it for me.

CHAPTER 20
On the Move

1962-1963
Granite Falls, Minnesota

The plan to move to Minnesota had come up suddenly. We would barely have time to get settled before school started. We were Kansas City kids plunked down in the middle of the prairie because Dad's company had decided to expand the feed business to the farmers of southwestern Minnesota. We spent the final days of summer packing our belongings in boxes and labeling them TO MINNESOTA. But when it came down to it, very little actually made the trip with us. Mom and Dad, eleven kids (one more on the way) had to fit in Dad's new pickup truck.

Minnesota is where Mom grew up. It made sense in a way to make the move. Grandpa and Grandma Meldahl had retired to the area. Grandpa found a home outside of Granite Falls for us to rent. It had stood empty for a few years, but it was the largest farmhouse in the area. And it just happened to be on the edge of our Dad's new sales territory.

We moved into that farmhouse the day before Labor Day. The landlord called his empty house, the "showpiece of the county." Some showpiece, it was overrun with mice and squirrels. There was a dead raccoon and a live snake in the basement. But we didn't have much time to get settled; school started the day after we moved in and snow came in October. It wasn't even winter yet.

By our second winter we had experienced blizzards and below-zero and back country roads ending in a wall of snow. Thanksgiving was a sad time. President Kennedy had just been assassinated and Dad left the house that Friday afternoon to buy a TV so we could watch "history in the making," as he kept saying all weekend long. Our old TV sat in a garage in Kansas City with a mountain of our other possessions, the ones that weren't able to fit in the truck when we moved. The ones Dad was always promising to retrieve "next month." He had been saying that for so many months, I held out hope it meant we'd be moving back to Kansas City. The farmers of Minnesota had not been very receptive to a new way of feeding their livestock. Dad's sales career stalled. He wasn't used to that; he could sell anything to anybody. But not here. Not in Minnesota.

Christmas was memorable only because of Kevin's red truck. It had started out to be a thin Christmas with Dad's delayed commission check. Mom spent December with her Bernina sewing machine creating gifts out of yards of flannel fabric. But how to fill the space beneath a crooked Christmas tree is what concerned me. I challenged her in that newly teenage sass of mine. "Mom, the little kids need toys, not pajamas!"

Little Kevin had earmarked a red fire engine in the Sears catalogue. He prayed for it quietly at night in the bathroom so the others wouldn't tease him. I overheard his prayers but had not told Mom until now. "Don't you worry, dear." Mom pulled out a charge card from her purse. Somehow, a mom with no paycheck and 12 kids, had finagled a line of credit from Sears. "Don't tell your father!"

When Kevin's shiny red truck appeared under the Christmas tree it made you want to believe again. We were 12 kids that Christmas morning screaming and squealing and creating a mountain of wrapping paper that spilled into the hallway.

Days later on a highway to Minneapolis an out-of-control speeding vehicle crashed into our lives. It happened so fast this undoing. One. By. One.

I would awaken in an unfamiliar bed in the middle of the night. I would agonize over where my baby sister was. Before Christmas Beth had taken to crawling out of her crib and burrowing under my covers. I would change her wet diaper and we'd snuggle till morning.

But who was now watching over her on the dark winter nights?

Our parents had no idea
the full weight of the bullet
we dodged that day.

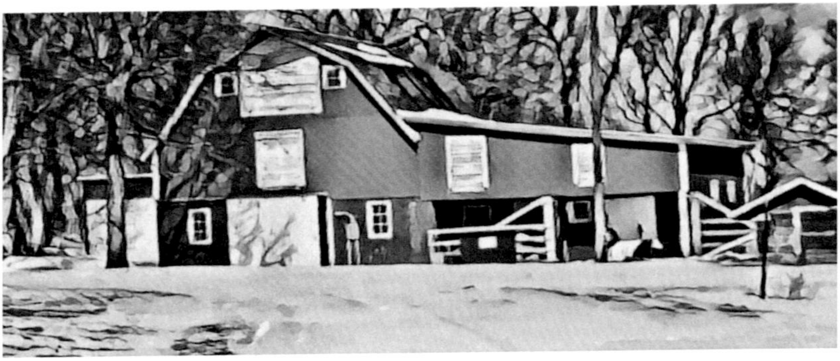

CHAPTER 21
The Aftermath

Spring, 1964

75 days.

That's how long it took.
Beth had her first birthday without us.
Kevin turned 7.
They say time slows down when you're afraid.
75 nights since the accident.
We measured our lives based on what happened before and after ... before *the accident* ... after *the accident* ... on the day of *the accident*. I'm not sure why we always referred to it as *the accident*. Maybe it seemed a softer way to say it, as if it could cushion the aftermath of the crash.

An accident is a misfortune, a fluke. Something that happens by chance. But the car crash was more than misfortune. It was a torpedo of metal barreling down a highway, ignoring a stop sign, blowing past a yield sign before colliding with the Chevy's destiny. There were no tire marks on the pavement to indicate the driver even tried to stop.

It was not chance that put an unlicensed teenager behind the wheel. It was not a fluke he was driving a delivery vehicle that morning. The evidence showed the teenagers made bakery deliveries before school. Perhaps they were running late.

The full force of their hurtling bread truck hit right where Mom was sitting. No wonder they called it a miracle that she survived. And like *accident*, the word *miracle* became another complicated word for me.

A miracle would have been our parents returning to us that night back in January.

75 times 12 kids: 900 night-times of confusion, anxiety, foreboding.

It was supposed to be 68 days. Mom had fully come out of her coma and was making good progress, enough to continue recuperating at home. The doctors thought her outlook would brighten if she could be surrounded by her kids. In mid-March the doctors discharged Mom and an ambulance brought her to Granite Falls. The plan was for her to be checked into the local hospital overnight and then Dad could take her home. The foster families had agreed to deliver us to the farm that Saturday morning.

But on the outskirts of town the County Sheriff turned on his lights and stopped the ambulance. He motioned for the driver to pull into the Granite Falls Motel parking lot. That's when he had to deliver the bad news. Our house had just been condemned, declared a health hazard. The sheriff checked on the house that morning and discovered the furnace had run out of oil, perhaps weeks earlier. All the pipes had frozen and it could take a week or more to fix it.

There was some dispute about jurisdiction of the ambulance and the two hospitals. In that parking lot on the edge of town a battle ensued between the various parties. The local hospital did not want to admit Mom. Dad rushed to the parking lot to see if he could rent a motel room, but the ambulance driver refused to release Mom, said he had no option but to turn around and take her the 70 miles back to the Glencoe hospital.

Our memories are foggy about that almost-reunion. Paul remembers a classmate telling him there was a commotion up on the hill. An ambulance and a squad car and a man hollering in the parking lot.

It was a bleak week for all of us, but finally, on day 75, the pipes were fixed and the house was ready for Mom. It was our Easter *miracle*.

Dad made a hurried trip around town picking up all of us kids so we could be at our house to welcome Mom.

We spent the morning transforming the living room into a bedroom. Mom wouldn't be able to navigate stairs for some time.

Mrs. Wengert drove to Glencoe to bring Mom home. No more crazy ambulance rides. Karl and Eric carried Mom into the house. She had a long cast on her left arm from her shoulder to her fingertips. She couldn't put weight on her left leg. Dad set up the wheelchair and we all screamed our welcome when he pushed her into the living room. Mom wore dark glasses to cover up her damaged eye and a scarf to hide the bald spots from stitches in her head. Baby Beth stayed close to my side and cried when I took her near Mom's wheelchair.

Mom turned away and I could tell she was crying. Our exciting homecoming quickly turned quiet and uncomfortable. Dad told Eric and John to make sandwiches and soup for lunch while Andy and Paul lifted Mom into her living room bed. Dad shushed the rest of us and ushered us out of the room. He called a family meeting in the kitchen.

"You all need to be extra careful the next few days. Your mother just spent three months in a room by herself and she needs peace and quiet. Understood?"

"Yes, Daddy," we whispered.

"Who's missing?"

"Karl and Kevin," said Andy. "I saw them heading to the barn."

"Go get them. I want everyone in the house together."

Eric and Andy and I ran to the barn. The snowfort was long gone, faded into the muddy field leaving only a discarded broomhandle and a tattered handkerchief.

The field where we built our snowfort was called an *aftermath*, the foreman at the farm had told us last fall. He called it a field of second chances. "The land gives us two wheat crops in one year. If all goes well."

But the next field over, behind the barn, was not so lucky. Winter snows came too early, rendering the cornfield impossible to harvest. The farmer taught us another term: *overwinter*. He was forced to overwinter his corn. "The yield will be lower," he explained, "but corn can survive till the spring. You wait and see."

What we could see on this spring day was a bleak array of dead-looking cornstalks. Behind the barn Karl and Kevin had left easy footprints in the muddy snow. We followed their tracks clear across rows of dried and brittle stalks to the opposite edge of the field, our shoes fat with mud. The row was littered with corncobs.

Kevin was shivering and whimpering as Karl sliced and jabbed at the tallest cornstalk with his pocketknife. "Do you see this? Look at this!"

"Karl, put that knife away. What is wrong with you?"

"I sleep with this knife and you know why? Someday I'll be doing this." He stabbed another cornstalk. "Every day I search for that bread-truck driver. I look for him wherever I go. Someday I will meet up with him. And so help me God, I'm going to kill him. I'm going to make him pay for what he did to us."

Kevin's body shook from his sobbing. "Karl! Stop it."

"Look at him," screamed Karl. "He can't find the red fire engine. His Christmas present. Father Buckley said the kids couldn't take any toys with them. We ran out here and hid it that day. And now we can't find it, goddammit."

Eric wrapped his arms around Kevin.

"And that's not all! That old man where Kevin had to live? He made Kevin help with the paper route."

"I didn't mind," said Kevin hiccuping through his sobs. "I saw Katy in the window so I rang the doorbell. Karen was there too!"

"At least he could see them once a week," I said. "I never knew where they were."

"No, dammit. The old man came after Kevin screaming and smacking him upside the head and told him never to do that again. Our brother had to deliver the Sunday paper every single goddam week to that house and he could not even speak to his own sisters."

"But I did wave to them," Kevin added. "I did it and I never got caught. I did like this," and Kevin showed us how he carried the paper in one hand and kept his other arm extended in front of him and moved his hand up and down at the wrist, a stiff sort of down-low wave. "Katy and Karen were always waiting at the window and only they saw me do it."

"Every single goddam week. Kevin never dared to ring the doorbell. Where our sisters were! All because of that drunken old man, who ushers at church every Sunday. God damn him. God damn them all to hell."

"Karl! That's enough!" I had never heard him swear. Ever. "We need to get back. It's time for lunch."

Karl refused to leave the field. Eric hoisted Kevin on his back and followed Andy to the house. I ran to get Dad and sent him into the cornfield. It was almost suppertime when they emerged, Karl clutching a rusty toy truck.

"Here you go, Kevin. We'll get some red paint and fix it up. We'll make it like new. I promise."

That night before bedtime, we all gathered in the living room, hovering around Mom's bed. "Pay attention, everyone," Dad bellowed. "For now we will be saying our nightly prayers in this room." Everyone scrambled to find places around Mom and Dad's big bed. "Put the youngest here on the foot of the bed, but no bouncing. Everyone else kneel down."

I looked up and studied Mom's face. An angry scar sliced her nose, cutting over to the side of her cheek. More stitches had crisscrossed her forehead, following her hairline on the left and down to her chin. She wore sunglasses all that first day, covering up her droopy left eye. I got up and gingerly began to take her glasses off.

"Patsy, don't."

But she didn't resist. I reached in my pocket and pulled out her handkerchief with the crocheted trim, the one I had carried for 75 days, and draped it over her eye. I turned off the lamp closest to her face. The room took on a softer glow as warm tears began to caress my cheeks.

Beth crawled across the bed and put her head delicately on Mom's stomach.

Dad stood looking out the picture window, for a long time it seemed. Finally he took a deep breath and began to pray:

"We are blessed to be together once again and let us be thankful for this miracle. Let us thank those who helped us these past several weeks. And, Dear Lord, help us grant forgiveness to those who harmed us. Kids, how many times does Jesus tell us we must forgive? Not 7 times, but ..."

We knew the answer. "70 times 7!"

"Correct. That's what we are called to do. Let's begin: Now I lay me down to sleep ..." We all joined in unison, until the "God bless" part. But we weren't praying with the same innocent abandon as before.

"God bless Mommy," Dad started.

"God bless Mommy," was our tempered refrain. "God bless Daddy," we repeated after him and on down the line. "God bless Karl ... Patsy ... Eric ... Andy ... John ... Paul ... Kevin ... Katy ... Karen ... Phillip ... Jimmy ... Beth."

"Amen."

"Wait," said Dad, still staring out the picture window. "We need to do this." He took a deep breath and looked directly at Karl. "And God bless the driver of that bread truck."

No one repeated him in this unexpected request. This forgiveness stuff was not easy. How could we pray for someone who had done this to us? Karl glared at Dad.

Then Phillip, who never spoke without prompting, piped up in his small voice, his dimples deepening, "God bless the red truck!"

Dad jerked around to find Phillip and stared at him for a second, then burst out laughing. "Well, I'll be darn. God bless the red truck!"

We all chimed in. "God bless ... the red truck!"

Dad bent down stiffly and patted Phillip's head, telling him he was a smart cookie for a three-year-old. I looked around the room counting ... 12, 13, 14. Karl had buried his head in the quilt by Mom's cast. His shoulders were shaking. Mom reached over with her good hand and stroked his hair.

Our overwintering had ended. We had come home.

CHAPTER 22
A Full House

Summer, 1964

We reunited in the spring and by summer we were on the move again, eager to leave Granite Falls behind. As a family we were cautiously trying to find a way back to each other. The farmhouse could not be that place.

Our homecoming always felt fragile. Mom and Dad were now considered disabled, and caseworkers would come to the door checking, monitoring, judging. It seemed the Authorities were ready to declare them unfit parents. It was a fear always hanging over our heads.

Mom became a taskmaster at making us pick up after ourselves. She had always been the easier parent; Dad was the drill sergeant. "You never know when someone from the County might stop by," Mom would now scold. Years ago Dad had drawn up a poster of rules for how the dishes got stacked, washed, dried, and put away. After every meal. "Just like they do in the Army," he would say. Beds were made before school except on Tuesdays, when the sheets got washed. The rest of the day, throughout the house, Mom let us have our chaos. By lights out, the house was put back together and ready for the next days' onslaught.

But after Mom got home from the hospital she learned from Mrs. Brennen that people thought she was a sloppy housekeeper. Mrs. Brennan told her when the church people came the day of the accident, a Tuesday, they made note of all the sheets and diapers and clothes in a heap in the back stairwell. They saw dirty dishes and spilled food on the kitchen table. They assumed that's how we lived all the time, not seeing it for what it was—a snapshot of the daily chaos that would have disappeared when Karl cleaned up after naptime. But for the accident ...

Then the furnace had run out of oil sometime in February or March, no one knew for sure. The house was deemed uninhabitable. Dad had to break the news to us that we would have to spend another week in foster care.

The Wengerts hired a crew to clean up the mess from the broken waterpipes and make the house livable again. Karl and Eric helped every day after school. Dad told the oil delivery guy, "To hell with filling the oil tank, just put in the smallest amount to get the furnace up and running for a few more weeks." He knew we'd be gone before it turned cold next winter. For some reason the furnace running out of oil became a checkmark against him. But for the accident ...

Mom would be facing many surgeries and follow-up medical care. Dad wanted us to live closer to a hospital. During Mom's recuperation, doctors had often said: "If only we could get her to a Minneapolis hospital, or better yet the Mayo Clinic." But they didn't want to risk moving her.

Dad's boss had kept his job open. As long as we were in the vicinity of his sales territory, we could choose to live anywhere. A salesman only needs a car and a clear voice, Dad would say. He should have added a strong back, because his was still in bad shape. Driving long distances was challenging, even though he wore a stiff cumbersome back brace.

Until Dad could return to work we were living on an insurance fund from the lawsuit that was in the works. An attorney at the truck stop in Glencoe approached Dad one day. He had heard about the accident—it was the talk of the town. Mr. Aitchinson made a lot of promises and followed up with a lot of phone calls on our behalf. He even wrote an impassioned letter to Governor Rolvaag, who responded months later. Mr. Aitchinson was certain the insurance company would have to award a huge sum of money. Unprecedented circumstances, he called it. A jury would be moved by a family of kids with a disabled mom, he would argue to the adjusters, especially since the vehicle involved belonged to a business. But Dad was pressured by Grandpa and others to settle early, so there would be no groundbreaking lawsuit. We would learn the hard way about legal wranglings and failed promises.

Dad thought Minneapolis was too big a place to raise a family. St. Cloud had the Catholic angle with its many churches and schools, and our parents wanted us kids back in Catholic schools, so that seemed like the logical first step. Rochester had the Mayo Clinic and that was also a good possibility.

Our parents convened a family meeting the night before the first house-hunting trip. We all got to state our opinion on where we should move. Karl voted for another farm, but far away. Maybe near a lake, said John. Kevin wanted to be able to walk to a store.

"Kansas City," was my answer.

Mom felt strong enough to go along on the weekend trips to scope out a new home. She was propped up in the back seat of the car with pillows and pain pills. Andy and John got to go—Andy to ride shotgun and read the map, John to sit in the back to help Mom.

Their plan was to drive to Hutchinson, stop for lunch, and get to St. Cloud in time for a meeting with a priest Dad had met in the hospital. The priest had promised to show them homes for rent.

When I watched them leave the driveway that first Saturday after our reunion I got that cold disturbance in my chest again. From then on I would feel it every time they left in a car. Every. Single. Time.

They never made it to the afternoon meeting with the priest in St. Cloud. According to Dad, who loved to retell this story, on the outskirts of a little town, Mom told him to stop the car. She didn't know why, she just wanted him to stop.

Dad pulled over beside the highway sign announcing the next town:

BIRD ISLAND
Pop. 1,384

"What an odd name for a town," Mom noted. "Let's stop here for coffee." Dad eased back onto the highway, scanning ahead. Halfway through town, there it was, "like it was waiting for us—*The Coffee Cup Café.*"

It was mid-morning and the café was almost empty. Except for one boisterous man who came over before the waitress had time to pour coffee. "I'm Charlie Nienow. Welcome to Bird Island, the classiest town in a hundred miles. You must have noticed our wide paved streets. Most small towns can't say the same."

Dad was hooked, impressed by this guy's cheerleading. One salesman to another.

"What brings you to our lovely little city?"

"We are on our way to St. Cloud. My business is moving me to the area. We've been living on a farm in Granite Falls. Now we want to get our kids back in Catholic schools."

"Well, hold on a darn minute. Have I got something to show you."

Within an hour, Mr. Nienow had heard our story and was ready to lead a tour. The first stop was St. Mary's Catholic Church. Dad had noticed the tall steeple from miles away. Equally impressive was the church itself, two schools, a rectory and a convent.

Within another hour, Mr. Nienow had drawn up a purchase agreement on an abandoned house one-half block off Main Street, across from the Methodist Church and three blocks from our new school.

For $4,500 Dad bought us a home. The house was built at the turn of the century, and looked like it. People complained about it being the town eyesore—hadn't been painted in over fifty years. Giving life to abandoned houses had become a pattern for us. The convent, the farmhouse, and now this antique. Mr. Nienow knocked $500 off the purchase price because Dad promised to start painting and fixing up the outside first.

The inside was a puzzle. Two elderly sisters had lived there for years but there were no electrical outlets on the main floor. Snakes of extension cords hung from the ceilings and lined the staircase to the second floor, where there were live outlets.

That's where the electricity came into the house. Mr. Nienow could not explain why no one ever bothered to wire the house to code. Every bit of it was jerry-rigged. So much of the house was a patchwork of unfinished projects and problems, the uneven floors, the dirt cellar, a barely working furnace. The one tiny bathroom did not have a bathtub, just a rusted old shower stall. Included in the purchase was a slanted garage that never housed a car. The best feature of all was an extra lot beside the house that became our playground. It was a perfect size for baseball in the summer and football in the fall, an ice skating rink in the winter.

Everyone but Mom and me loved this new town. So much for moving to a city. Bird Island—which wasn't an island—was smaller than Granite Falls, by over a thousand people.

Eventually Mom came to accept it and even grew to love it. I was always the harder sell. The jerry-rigged house didn't help. Dad knew I was disappointed and tried to soften the blow that we were moving to a town nowhere near a city. The day after buying the house the plan was to return with a carload of boxes and Dad asked just me to go with him.

In each small town along the way he pointed out how narrow the streets were. When we got to Bird Island he made a point to drive me around town to showcase its good points.

"Look, there's a tennis court. We don't have that on the farm. Over there's an indoor roller skating rink and people come from all over for the County Fair."

"Where's the island?" I asked.

Soon enough the town ran out of itself and Dad turned back to Main Street. We stopped in front of the post office. It was explained that all the townspeople came here to get their mail. Every day but Sunday. There was a wall of numbered boxes that could be opened with a combination. Ours was #21, F-H-F. We got back in the car and at the corner Dad made a right turn and pointed towards an alley. "Through those trees, you can see our new home. Look how close it is to come and get the mail. No one but you and me have the combination."

I strained to see through the trees but I couldn't see the house. Dad unexpectedly sped up and drove quickly through two blocks, turned right again and parked in front of St. Mary's church. I was confused.

"Let's go in and light a candle. To bless our new home. Then I'll take you there."

The church was tall and stately, at least three times larger than the one we were leaving behind. Dad reached for my arm as he struggled to climb the steps. His back was really acting up today, he said. Inside, the church was dark and silent, except far down the aisle by a side altar, little flickers of light from candles seemed to be calling us. It was so rare to get Dad all to myself I wanted this moment to slow down so I could savor it. I can still hear the sound a quarter makes as it plinks into the metal coin holder. The flash of fire as the match flares. The sweet smell of burning beeswax. I wanted to tell Dad about the dozen candles I lit for him on his birthday, but something stopped me. It was the beginning of our not-talking-about what we had just lived through.

I should have known that Dad had been working up his courage to show me the house. When he finally stopped the car on 8th Street, I had to stifle a gasp. The sight of the tall narrow house sucked the breath right out of me. Dad started unloading the boxes but I couldn't move. He came over to open my door.

"You'll be able to walk to school, honey. No more waiting for the bus. Look at these wide streets. We'll bring the bikes next trip."

I fought back tears. I wanted to cheer up for Dad, he was trying so hard. But in front of me stood a shabby, haunted house.

"And this time, we own the ground underneath all that prairie sky. This house will look so different with a coat of paint. I promise."

A month later on one of the final moving trips Dad pulled over on the shoulder and stopped the car. He asked me to stand under the highway sign so he could take a Polaroid picture. "Look at that, will you? Tomorrow, when we officially move here, our family will push the population to 1,400. I think that's a good sign, a nice round number."

"Um, Dad, my math says: 1,398."

"Oh, honey, those population counts come from the 1960 census. Don't you think the town has grown by a couple more residents since then?"

The next day Dad stopped at the edge of town and over Mom's objection handed Paul a pencil. Karl hoisted Paul on his shoulders and he penciled in the new population count. Nobody but us would know it was there. Over the years Dad delighted in telling people that our family increased the population of Bird Island to 1,400. Sometimes he exaggerated even more and said it was 1,500. Because, you know, the new census would someday show that.

The walls of our new home must have held many stories but we quickly paneled and painted over them all. This house was smaller than the farmhouse and much smaller than the convent. The one tiny bathroom for 14 people became the first challenge. Dad drew up plans to convert one of the downstairs bedrooms to a big bathroom. He envisioned a roomy shower stall, like you'd find in a locker room, so four or five boys could shower at once.

For some reason Dad loved cement. You'd think after what happened to Andy, he'd not want to fool around with a cement mixer but it was in his blood. He loved everything about it, the forming, the mixing of sand and aggregate, the furious nature of the pour when everything happened at once, and finally the troweling and curing and waiting for the permanence.

Dad loved it so much he had several concrete projects in mind. The driveway would be an obvious one and the front and back steps. But his first project he brought *into* the house. Our bathroom is where he started. He divided the room down the middle—one-half would be the wood floor, the other half a concrete slab, six inches high, that would surround the bathtub with space for a separate walk-in shower. The bathtub would appear sunken, like an in-ground pool. Dad said it was so Mom could step in easier, his version of a handicapped bathtub. He even experimented with adding color to the cement so it dried to a soft shade of mauve.

Cementing the floor of the bedroom-turned-bathroom made the shower like those you'd find in a gym. Several strategically placed drains kept the boys' shower water from ruining the rest of the wood floor. Theoretically.

On the day of the concrete pour we all had to be ready to put our handprints in the setting concrete, marking our place in the world, before it hardened.

Every house we lived in had a concrete imprint of our presence.

While Dad worked on the bathroom. Eric and I climbed up the extension ladders the hardware store owner had delivered to the side of the house. Mr. Bohm told us to be extra careful. If we didn't get the ladders too marked up we could return them. Fat chance. Karl was afraid of heights, so Eric and I were charged with painting the highest points. Karl painted the lower boards and refilled our paint cans and accidently-on-purpose splashed us with his full brush. The boards soaked up paint like a thirsty beast. Two coats and you could barely see any progress.

The first Sunday in our new town I sat on the front porch steps enjoying a break from painting. This was a peaceful, almost sleepy street. Once an hour, maybe, a car or two would slowly cruise by. Later we would realize the slowly cruising cars were eyeing all the new commotion at the abandoned house. It was the talk of the town.

Our street was lined with a boulevard of leafy trees forming a canopy overhead, softening the summer sun. I didn't want to admit it yet—there were some good things about the town.

On the ground around me the grass and bushes were splotched with white spots. Dad didn't care that we were sloppy housepainters. He said we could just mow the grass, and the paint spills would magically disappear. Mom wished we'd be more careful and not ruin the peony beds. Sal, the neighbor, had already run over to mention the bushes were hers, even though they were inside our property line.

Each day the outside of the house was starting to look a little better. But the siding was so starved of paint it would take us the rest of the summer to complete the job. No matter how hard we tried, this house would never be more than a freshly painted eyesore.

Our neighbor Sal had already taken to coming over every day to have morning coffee with Mom. She brought her own coffee pot and you might think she was being neighborly, but Dad thought she was nosy. She was quick to tell us the latest stories going around town. Most of it was about our family.

"I've heard it said," Sal would begin. "You really have 13 children. The story is you keep one locked upstairs in the attic."

"This has got to be the most ridiculous thing I've ever heard," Mom laughed. "We don't even have an attic."

"Oh, yes, you do," Sal corrected her. "It's upstairs in the back closet. You pull on this cord and a ladder comes down."

Mom was in a lot of pain, but she made Sal follow her upstairs to prove that no child was living in an attic we didn't even know was there.

Another day, Sal had another story. "People are saying that some of your children are adopted. They aren't all yours?"

"My dear Sal," Mom started, "I can describe to you in great detail each and every labor pain I had with each and every baby. Would you like me to begin with Karl? He's the first."

"Oh, no, I don't believe those rumors. I'm just the messenger."

Sal was prickly on the outside, but Mom thought she was a promising good neighbor, maybe a little touched in the head with all her crazy stories about us. It took all summer but we eventually won Sal over. Probably because most of our activities took place on the other side of the house—Gertie's side. There was nothing but bushes on Sal's side.

That first Sunday we got to take a break from painting. I had gone to early Mass and now it was mid-morning and already oppressively hot. I had changed from my Sunday clothes to a bathing suit and was helping Karl set up the sprinkler so we could cool off. I noticed the neighbor lady's curtains moving. Gertie could see into our backyard from her kitchen window. I grabbed one of Dad's white shirts off the clothesline to use as a cover-up. Having neighbors nearby took some getting used to, after living on a farm.

A big black walnut tree blocked Gertie's view of our front steps, so that's where I found privacy. Across the street was a quiet Methodist church, with stained-glass windows. I hadn't seen anyone coming or going all week, so I felt comfortably unnoticed on the porch steps. Without warning a line of cars and pickups began to stop in front of our house, turning the street into a parking lot. As if on cue, the vehicles pivoted and parked diagonally.

All the streets were wide in this town, as we already knew, and except for Main Street, all the cars parked parallel to the curb.

But today was different, and every Sunday thereafter we witnessed the dance of the parking cars. That morning every churchgoer turned and stared at me in my Dad's shirt before entering the big wooden church doors. One kindly lady hollered, "Good morning, neighbor!"

I had never met a Methodist before and I imagine the Methodists were startled to see a bunch of kids in the house across the street. After the two Peterson sisters moved away, no one lived in the house. There had been no children on the entire block. There were no Nancys or Stevens or Jerrys. All our neighbors had old-people names—Gertie and Sal and Hazel. Soon though, sleepy 8th Street transformed into a block where the kids took over.

To escape the stares of the churchgoers, I nudged the screen door open and quietly slipped through, careful not to let the door bang shut. I sat down low on one of our moving boxes and from my hiding place I could stare back.

I noticed a guy hurriedly running towards our street from the next block. At the church entrance he crouched down to tie his shoe and when he stood up he towered over a lady with a cane. I watched him usher in the last churchgoer and close the big wooden doors behind him.

The sound of the organ and muffled singing drifted across the street. This music was not familiar to me but it had a churchy cadence. I figured it would be safe to go back to my perch on the steps, during the service anyway. Paul brought me a glass of ice water. I scooted over so he could sit beside me. Paul wanted to show me his new baseball glove. He kept pounding his fist into the palm of the stiff leather. "This will help break it in properly," he said. "My coach told me."

Dad had enrolled all the boys in summer baseball camps. He knew it would be a way for them to make friends before school started in the fall. I would start swimming lessons soon.

Bird Island had become a little famous, according to Mr. Charlie Nienow, for having the sense to build the first and only indoor pool between here and Minneapolis. Another plus for the town.

Out of nowhere, a chocolate-brown bundle of fur bounded across the wide street weaving in between the cars, finally stopping at my feet. A panting puppy looked up at me with pleading eyes. I picked him up and he flopped into my lap resting his head on Paul's leg. We sat without speaking, Paul and me, stroking the puppy's sleepy head. He licked the ice from my glass and let out a big sigh.

We sat like that for the longest time. I was imagining this puppy was a stray and hoping he could become ours. I even began to think of possible names. Danny-Boy seemed fitting and I began to hum Dad's favorite Irish tune and Danny-Boy fell asleep.

The organ blasted a boisterous song: the same tall boy propped open the church doors. He looked to be Karl's age, maybe older. The bundle of fur in our lap jolted up and yipped a puppy bark. Before we could stop him, he dashed across the street.

"Dudley, how did you get out?" the guy playfully scolded the dog as he picked him up. Then he looked in our direction and waved.

Paul whispered to me, "That's my baseball coach!" He was too timid to wave back, and because Paul and I had our shyness in common we both jumped up and ran inside the house to escape the stares from any more Methodists.

One day it would become clear that many meaningful people came into our lives in this unlikely place.

But for the accident ...

When I started school in the fall as a freshman I would learn the name of Paul's coach. Tom was also a freshman. Our senior year he would be chosen Captain of the football team. That spring he would ask me to the prom.

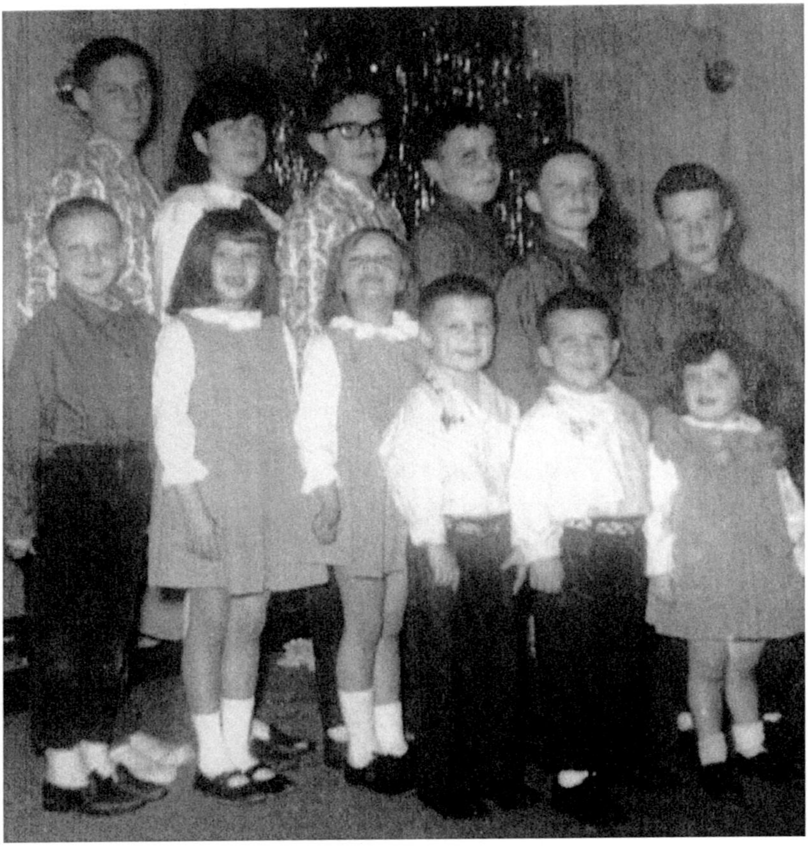

CHAPTER 23
The Last House

1964-1968

None of us could know it then, how Bird Island would be our final landing place, the final space that would shelter all 14 of us. We still claimed all that prairie sky, but in Bird Island we had our plot of land to ground us.

The summer of 1964 marked the beginning of our mending years. We never talked about the accident. Mom had scars across her face and often had a cast on her arm or leg, depending on which reconstructive surgery the Mayo doctors were attempting, so sometimes the accident had to be mentioned. But as kids we never talked about our time apart, in the foster homes—not with each other, not to our parents, definitely not to our classmates.

We learned to seal off the feelings connected to that time. But no adult thought to ask us either—no relative, no teacher, no clergy. Kids are tough, they would say. They bounce back. Our motto had become: No one died. We all survived.

Dad's scars were on the inside and insomnia became his nightly companion. It was something we had in common. Sometimes I'd awaken before dawn and carefully tiptoe down the creaky steps and find him at the dining room table writing furiously on a legal pad. He called it "chicken scratching." His penmanship was so bad, "even I can't read it half the time," he'd laugh. Dad preferred sitting at his Royal typewriter pecking out with one finger what was in his mind to write. The typewriter was on a desk in the bedroom and the noisy keys would have disturbed Mom, so Dad would wait until later to transcribe his scribblings.

He would often shout from his desk: "Patsy, come and help me decipher this. What did I mean to say?"

He would write one of many passionate letters to the editor, or a senator, or the governor. Mom's family were friends of Vice President Hubert Humphrey back when he was mayor of Minneapolis. Even though Dad didn't care for him, or vote for him, he wrote many letters to him. Dad proudly served in World War II but he didn't want his sons going off to a useless war in the jungles of Vietnam. He hoped his letters could help change Humphrey's stance on the war.

One night Humphrey was speaking in a nearby town. Mom wanted to go to see her childhood acquaintance. Grandpa was still active in politics and got tickets. Dad stubbornly stood in the back by the door, "so I could easily bolt if necessary." Dad further explained, "I go in shaking my head No to everything he said, but before long that son-of-a-bitch had me nodding Yes!" Dad marveled for days at Humphrey's beguiling speech. "He's quite the talker; just wish he wasn't so far out there. But he's got moxie. I gotta give him that."

Dad and I had many endless debates during those sleepless times. I loved to spar with him. We rarely agreed on current events, but Dad taught me how to switch sides in the midst of a discussion to keep an argument alive. It allowed me to understand another's point of view, even if I ended up disagreeing with him still.

Dad was a contradiction—conservative in many political beliefs but always intrigued by new causes. He and I sparred over the emerging women's movement. "A woman's place is in the home, otherwise, who would raise the children?"

"But, Dad, you don't want me to stay home. You want me to be a journalist."

"That's different. You are different."

"I'm not different, Dad. Your argument is weak." He was teaching me well. I had become Dad's conundrum.

The summer before college he would pour over my school syllabus and point out classes I should take. Philosophy was the most important subject, Dad thought, and next was world religions. To me that was the paradox of our father. He was such a devoted Catholic, but he thought it important to study all religions.

In those pre-dawn talks we had Dad showed me several pages he had written about his life and our family. He asked me to finish it if he were unable. One morning that summer Mom joined us at the table. When Dad got up to make her coffee, she whispered, "You don't have to become a journalist to write stories. That's your Dad's dream. Go write your own stories. But ... " Mom paused to make big sweeping gestures, "we've given you lots of rich material!"

"That you have, Mom. That you have."

For years Bird Island became our sanctuary of gentle lies, an anchor that let us start over without a past. Those years were treasured as a place we could pretend to be normal. And eventually we became what we pretended to be: normal.

Of course there would come a time for each of us to leave this town that had held us and healed us.

The summer of 1968 marked the beginning of our parting again. It was less of a rending this time. Karl got drafted into the Army and that fall I would go away to college. Two of us leaving at once was hard on our parents. My last week at home I caught Dad staring out of the dining room bay window. He'd call me over to say something but his lip would quiver and he'd raise his hand to wave me away. I tried not to show that I was excited for college, for I too felt their pain of my leaving.

On my last day at home I heard him whisper: "We dodged a bullet, Patsy. Four years ago, we dodged a bullet. Don't ever forget that."

It had been four years since the accident. Four years since Father Buckley tried to talk Dad into giving up some of the kids, tried to convince him a foster home was better than disabled parents.

I would not forget Dad's frantic car chase around Granite Falls that day of our reunion, racing like his life depended on it, like the life we had together depended on it. Dad came to the Grant's house first to pick me up. He honked and hollered frantically:

"We have to get every one of your brothers and sisters. Now!" I wasn't expecting him so early in the day, but I didn't ask questions. We were going home!

It's surprising how many kids you can tuck into a big sedan if there are no other options. John shared the front seat with me. I put my arm around his shoulder and he didn't move away, but he wouldn't look at me. This was the first time John and I had seen each other since I had to leave his foster home. Eric, Andy, Paul and Kevin squeezed in the back seat with the youngest on their laps: Katy and Karen and Phillip and Jimmy.

Beth was the last stop, a mile from our house. I ran up to the door. Mrs. Brennen shouted, "She's eating, I'll bring her over later." But Dad wasn't having it. Beth toddled to the door. The last time I saw her she was still my Baby Beth, crawling around the edge of the carpet. She had learned to walk without us. She let out a little squeal as I bent down to pick her up. Beth grabbed me around my neck and burrowed her head in my chest. I didn't remember her being so strong.

A baby changes the most in 75 days.

It was surprisingly quiet in that over-packed car. You could hear a voice in the backseat whimpering, the kind of shuddering, can't-catch-your-breath inhaling. I couldn't bear to turn around and see who it was. I think we all understood that sound, that shudder. Jimmy was sitting on Andy's lap. I heard Andy whisper: "It's OK, Jimmy, you don't have to cry anymore. We're going home!" Phillip had rested his head on the seat-back of the center console. His hair tickled my arm. His dimpled smile hurt my heart. Beth grabbed my cheeks and looked in my eyes, "Mama. Mama. Mama." It was almost overwhelming this jumbled mix of joy and hurt.

As we turned into the long driveway Dad gave us stern instructions. "Your mother isn't home yet, but she will be coming soon. You kids go run around the barn and shake off some of that bottled-up steam. She is going to need peace and quiet. Eric and Andy, make them run till they're out of breath. Patsy, come with me. I need to talk to Father. This won't take long. Got it?"

"Got it, Daddy," they all shouted back and tumbled out of the car.

I will never forget walking into the kitchen and seeing Karl drinking a cup of coffee with Father Buckley seated across from him.

It startled me. When did Karl start drinking coffee? Karl's hunting rifle was propped in the corner next to the back door. Not in its usual place, above the door, out of reach of young hands.

The kitchen was quiet. After an awkward moment, Dad said: "Thank you, Father, we'll take it from here." Just then all the kids, fresh from their run around the barn, blasted into the kitchen. Father Buckley had stood up.

"Mr. Kahmann, I hope you reconsider. We're only trying to think of the children."

"Karl, your manners, see Father to his car."

Dad and I stood together on the porch, watching Father's fancy car retreat down the long driveway and speed away. I could feel Dad's intense anger.

"We dodged a bullet today." I didn't quite understand what he meant. Later that night I would learn from Karl about what almost happened.

About how he had to keep Father Buckley at the kitchen table to prevent him from mobilizing some of the foster parents who wanted to adopt the child they had been taking care of. About how we almost didn't get our homecoming. This is what Karl told me:

≈

He and Dad were at the house early that morning because the house had to be inspected. The sheriff was coming to sign off on the paperwork, but Father Buckley's car showed up first.

"Something's not right, Karl," Dad said.

A few minutes later, the sheriff pulled in behind the priest. They walked together to the porch. Dad blocked the doorway. Finally, the sheriff said he needed to check the house. Dad stepped aside and both men came into the kitchen. Karl escorted the sheriff around the house. Neither Dad nor Father Buckley spoke. A few tense minutes later, the sheriff said the house was fine. With the signed order in hand, Dad walked the sheriff out to his car.

Father Buckley spoke, "I need to talk to your Dad, could you give us a moment?" Karl said he didn't leave the room. Father sat down at the kitchen table. Dad stood in the doorway.

"I'm in a hurry, Father, what brings you all the way out here?"

"Mr. Kahmann, some of us were talking ..."

"Who was talking?" Dad demanded.

"A few of the families taking care of your kids. With your wife still so injured and you too, we thought it best if some of the kids stay where they are."

"Are you out of your mind?!"

"Your wife is disabled. You can't possibly take care of all 12 ..."

Dad didn't let him finish: "Karl, where's your gun? Do ... not ... let ... him ... leave."

With that Dad limped-ran to the car—a big sedan, a rental courtesy of the insurance company. He had to get us kids home, before this got out of hand.

Karl made a pot of coffee as a way to keep Father from leaving. They had a pleasant conversation, but Father was insistent some of the kids would be better off not coming home. He asked him to convince our parents.

≈

"Karl!! Did Dad really tell you to get your rifle? You kept him here with your gun?"

"Not exactly, but it was nearby. Of course, I wouldn't have used it."

"Mom is doing so much better. She'll be walking soon. What could be the problem?"

It had never occurred to me there would be any question about us all coming home. Now I had a new worry. That first night of our reunion Beth had fallen asleep on my bed and rather than move her, I tucked in beside her, cherishing the peaceful sound of her breathing. I had prayed for the feel of this bed and Grandma's quilt for so many nights, but this new worry would keep me awake for many nights to come.

Still on the first day of our homecoming Dad was steadfast and that gave me a lifeline.

"Katy, bar the door," Dad had shouted, not to Katy but to all of us. "Nobody's getting past me again. I promise." It was his favorite expression when something remarkable happened.

Dad's obsession to honor his promise of keeping us together followed him to Bird Island. It kept him up at night. Mr. Aitchinson impressed on Dad how important it was to have a will. That was the only legal way to insure no one could separate us again. Mr. Aitchinson drew up the paperwork and agreed to act as our guardian. But when he died unexpectedly, Dad became desperate. Who could he trust now to keep 12 children together?

In the middle of a sleepless night, he found his answer. Minnesota State Statute, Section 517.02. There it was: Children were considered minors until age 21, with a curious exception. A girl could get married at 18 without her parents' permission. Dad pounded out this theory on his trusty typewriter with its temperamental keys. It followed logically, Dad typed, if a girl could get married, she could be a parent ... so why not a guardian? Karl was older by a year, but in 1968 the law wouldn't bend for him. He could be drafted into the Army, but legally he was still a minor.

That summer of 1968 Dad would drive to St. Paul to research his will project. Across from the Capitol at the State Law Library he met a newly graduated lawyer eager to assist pro bono.

I was to leave for the University of Minnesota in early September. Eric helped me carry my suitcases to the bus stop in front of the Coffee Cup Café.

Mom and Dad had wanted to show me a big send-off like they had done for Karl months before, but I couldn't bear to say goodbye in public. It was already planned they would come to see me in late October for parents' weekend.

I was determined to navigate the first weeks of college and the big city by myself. Minneapolis and St. Paul were sister cities, divided by the Mississippi River. They were referred to as *The Cities*. Our first home was also a sister city—Kansas City, Missouri and Kansas City, Kansas—with the Missouri River splitting them in two. Maybe that meant something.

Those first weeks I felt a confusing push and pull of emotions. An emerging desire for independence bumped up against our family's fragile past. A separate world was opening up to me but I'd quickly seesaw back to the house on 8th Street. Homesickness gripped me so hard I couldn't eat. On Sundays I would call home collect. When it was Beth's turn to talk I would ask her how she liked kindergarten. All she could do was cry and beg me to come home. There was no medicine in the world to fix this.

In late October as planned, Mom and Dad came to The Cities. They sent a cab to my dorm so I could join them at *The Lexington* where they were already celebrating. It was my 18th birthday. Bird Island was 100 miles and an era away from this ritzy restaurant. Dad had discovered it while researching in St. Paul.

The cab driver was a young hippy-looking guy, trying to hide his longish hair under a uniform cap. He fussed with the radio dial until a new song came on. "*Hey Jude*," he sang exuberantly. He talked about what it was like to be in the crowd at a Beatles' concert. The song was still playing when the cab screeched to a stop and the hippy cabbie jumped out to open my door. I could hear him singing, "*Na na na na-na-na na*," as I entered the restaurant where soft, jazzy music took over.

"Welcome to *The Lexington*," the doorman said while trying to take my coat, but I didn't understand the coat-check protocol and pushed my hands deep in my pockets. He pointed to a booth in the back. There was Dad waving a long piece of paper at me. A man I didn't recognize, his lawyer friend I presumed, sat next to him. There was Karl on leave from basic training. There was Mom holding onto his arm.

"Katy, bar the door," Dad hollered across the lounge. I figured I'd need to explain to the lawyer that I wasn't Katy.

I could tell this was Dad's kind of place—mahogany paneling offset with soft gaslights, a long robust bar, and "the best damn martini in 500 miles." It reminded Dad of his salesman days, before the accident, when his job took him to upscale restaurants in Chicago and New York.

Something about this tableau in the corner booth made me feel at home. I took off my coat.

Dad placed the legal-sized papers in front of me, pointing to my name in the Guardian Section. My parents were designating *me* the guardian of my ten younger siblings.

It was their Last Will and Testament, an unusual birthday present for a college freshman. With the stroke of a pen I became an adult. Sort of. I couldn't vote or drink alcohol, but I could legally parent a houseful of kids if called upon.

Dad raised a toast while the lawyer leaned over and whispered, "You're a loophole adult, and it might get challenged in court, but I'm here to fight for you."

I held the document up to the gaslight and stared at my name. This was the medicine we needed. "Sleep well tonight, Dad. No one's getting past us again."

The world breaks everyone and afterward many are strong at the broken places.
— **Ernest Hemingway**

EPILOGUE

Dad would never know the full weight of the bullet we had dodged that day.

In a distant future I would try to locate Father Buckley but I only found him in a newspaper story.* Father Gordon Buckley had been "credibly confirmed" as a pedophile priest. He would be banished from the priesthood and die before the court could reach him. His first victim to come forward was from Granite Falls, a boy from a "broken home" who lived across the street from the church.

This child was not his first victim. Father Buckley had been accused in other parishes. The pattern at the time was for the Bishop to quietly resettle "problem priests" to small towns in southwestern Minnesota. In Granite Falls Father Buckley had only been at St. Andrew's parish for two months before he put himself in charge of our family's upheaval. When our beloved neighbors, the Lutherans, had offered to come and stay with us to keep us together, Father Buckley chose to break us.

It all made sense now. For 75 days we were a broken family. But we dodged a bullet. We escaped Father Buckley despite his many ploys. Would Day 76 have been the tipping point?

I had a hard time finding my faith in church after that, but I am reminded that we did find new life in a benevolent field of second chances.

On Day 75 we all got to go home, strong at the broken places.

* http://www.granitefallsnews.com/article/2016022/NEWS/160229717 Database of Publicly Accused Priests in the United States: www.millerwilhry.com/priests/index.html

Father Gordon Buckley. Named publicly in 2/16 by the New Ulm diocese as having credible accusations of sexual abuse against him. Abuse said to have occurred at St. Andrew's in Granite Falls, where Buckley was assigned 1963-69.

POSTSCRIPT

Bird Island continued to be our homebase for many years. Dad never fully recovered from the accident. His broken back caused constant pain, but most of his injures were the invisible kind. Twelve years after our family reunited and moved to Bird Island, Dad died at age 52 of liver failure.

Mom made an astonishing recovery from her numerous injuries. In an experimental surgery on her crushed elbow, Mayo Clinic doctors gave her renewed mobility. They also created innovative glasses to correct her double vision. After Dad died, with four teenagers still at home, Mom got hired as a State coordinator, traveling to rural towns to set up resources for local unemployed residents.

Mom never remarried, telling us: when you've been with the love of your life, no one else holds a candle. Mom died in 1999, with all 12 adult children at her bedside. She had contracted pneumonia while traveling in Oregon. She died ten days later on Halloween, her favorite holiday. She was 75.

All 12 children have gone on to enjoy creative, productive lives. Though spread out across the country in 6 states and 1 Canadian province, we remain close.

Ten of us have married, 3 divorced, 1 widowed; 18 children born, 9 of 12 have become business owners; 5 earned college degrees working in these careers: teacher, lawyer, immigration officer, office manager, social worker, athletic trainer.

There is a 14-year age difference from the oldest to the youngest:

Karl moved to the remote wilderness of Canada and became a hunting and fishing guide, and an expert meatcutter and processor of moose meat for the local Native tribes. He is the local historian and storyteller. Lives at Jumbo's Cove, Ontario.

Patsy was awarded a journalism scholarship to the University of Minnesota, switched majors, eventually earning a degree in creative writing. While working on this manuscript part time, her career with the U of M Women's Basketball program provided another source of story material. 1 child. Lives in Edina, Minnesota.

Eric was awarded a scholarship to the University of Minnesota, married his high school classmate (a talented musician) and together they created a nationally sought-after arts and performance business. 2 children. Lives in Eden Prairie, Minnesota.

Andy learned printmaking at the *Bird Island Union*, working for over 55 years in the printing business as a head pressman, manager, owner; and now owns an antique letterpress printing company. 2 children. Lives in Montevideo, Minnesota.

John learned the craft of housebuilding, and became a sought-after superintendent for his expertise in building and remodeling hospitals; in retirement he continues to be sought-after with all the siblings for remodeling projects. Lives in St. Louis, Missouri.

Paul designed, and patented a popular jogging stroller, contracting with big-box stores, selling the business to a national corporation, retiring early; he continues to invent, patent and develop product businesses. 4 children. Lives in Bloomington, Minnesota, and Naples, Florida.

Kevin won a contract with the City of Minneapolis—the youngest business owner to do so—to repair curbs and sidewalks, currently owning a variety of successful national businesses. 4 children, 2 adopted. Lives in Bend, Oregon, and Jackson, Wyoming.

Katy earned degrees in Criminal Justice and Education, worked for the federal government—Customs and Border Protection—as an immigration officer; later earned a law degree and is a practicing immigration attorney. 3 children. Lives in Boston, Massachusetts.

Karen earned a degree in social work and developed a business of creative arts and performance classes for elementary students, and works for a world-wide technology company. 2 children. Lives in St. Louis, Missouri.

Phillip worked as the righthand man to the other siblings' businesses, sought after and fought over by the other siblings: construction, art shows, hunting and fishing guide. Lives in Edina, Minnesota, and spends as much time as possible at Jumbo's Cove, Ontario.

Jim earned a degree in the emerging field of athletic training and began his baseball career with the Montreal Expos. Hired by the Minnesota Twins, earned a 1991 World Series Ring, and became their Head Trainer. After 20 years in professional baseball, he continues a career in treating and rehabilitating professional athletes; is currently writing his memoir about his life in baseball. Lives in Tequesta, Florida.

Beth earned honors as a three-sport athlete in high school, had a stellar college career in basketball, and continued her love of sports in long distance running and mountain hiking, taught in Japan and Colorado, created a business helping those with traumatic brain injuries. Lives in Denver, Colorado.

ACKNOWLEDGMENTS

To Mom and Dad, this book is for you. It is my attempt to honor the legacy you left us. In all the ups and downs, during sweet and sorrowful times, you gave us the foundation of unconditional love. We knew at our core we were fiercely loved.

To my daughter Megan, I am so blessed and humbled to have you in my life. You have always been my touchstone to all that is good and beautiful. Thank you for your deep love and steadfast support.

To my granddaughter Genevieve, sweet G, you are such a blessing, and your spunky spirit graces me. I thank you for reading my chapters in progress and for the encouragement and feedback from those wise ten-year-old eyes.

To my brothers and sisters: Karl, Eric, Andy, John, Paul, Kevin, Katy, Karen, Phillip, Jim, and Beth. Of course I could not have told this story without you. I hope I have captured our shared experiences. Each of you could tell this from your eyes and it would be a different story, but I believe it would rhyme. Among us are a dozen views of our family history. This is mine.

To those foster families—the named and the unnamed—who took us in and gave us shelter, I express my sincere gratitude.

To my dear friend Samara Anjelae, talented writer and artist, thank you for believing in my story all those years ago and for your empathic encouragement. Thank you for bringing Wil Freebody of Long Island Recording Studio into this undertaking, and for his company's masterful audio recording of my chapters. I am grateful for our deep connections.

To my former husband Ross Alford, thank you for expanding my world through your gift of theatre. You were the first to believe in my writing. Your creativity and our collaborations set the stage for bringing these stories to life.

To my publishing team who generously read chapters and offered insightful edits, I hope you know how grateful I am: Julie Berg, Rita Reinecker, Sarah Koper, Becky Bohm, Lisa Childs, Tom Frazee, Genevieve Bergstrom. For the beautiful book cover, Jennifer Jones Nienaber. For your website wizardry, Julie Bonde. And A to Z Letterpress Printing, for taking this manuscript out of my hands and into the world!

To my award-winning filmmaking crew, thank you for showing me how to write and produce under impossible deadlines: Bill Bonde, Karen Bonde, Danielle Magnuson, Carla Kennedy.

To my fellow writing friends who have been with me from the beginning classes to the enduring, reassuring writing groups: Kris, Jenn, Marsha, Rachel, Jeanne, Kate, Tami, Rick; to the inspiring teacher and author Alison McGhee, my first writing teacher to honor a child's voice and let her speak.

To my work buddies at the University of Minnesota Athletics—the coaches, colleagues, student-athletes—who were my steadfast cheerleaders as I juggled writing stories in between navigating the crazy schedules: Dave Stomme, Ann Whittemore, Ted Riverso, Abby Kalland Kershaw, Barb Smith, Danny O'Bannion, Gary Wilson, Lindsay Whalen Greve, Janel McCarville, Nicole and Emily Oberlander. To so many more, I'll write that story one day!

A special thank you to friends who have seen me through the years when I couldn't write, but faithfully and always asked when I would finish those final chapters! Your loving persistence has been my North Star: Karen, Carla, Becky, Mary-Tree, Julie, Rita, Jim, Lynn, Linda, Dan, Cath, Lisa, Mark.

And finally, to a special band of Bird Island classmates, we only knew each other briefly years ago. With our recent reconnection, you have been instrumental in urging me, encouraging me to finish! I am grateful for the synchronicity that brought us back together. With heartfelt thanks to the Peterson twins, Diane Anderson and Denise Kienholz, Nancy (Dahlgren) Nordin, Steve Flann, Jerry Beckman, Dan Nordin, and for your bold deadline, Tom Frazee.